Big Waves, Small Boat, Two Kids

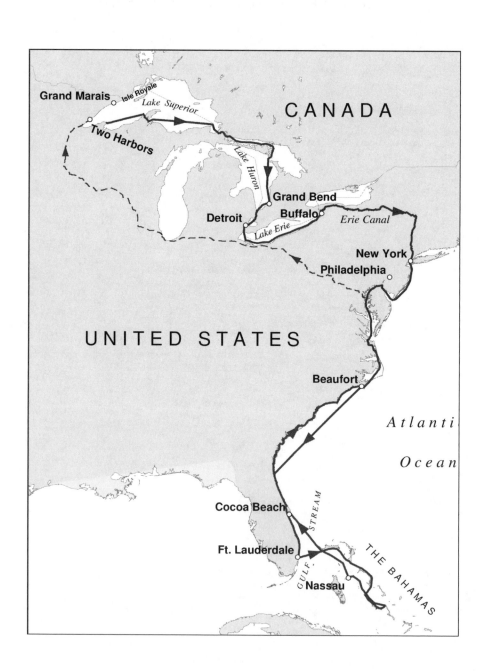

Big Waves, Small Boat, Two Kids

A Family Sailing Adventure

Katya Goodenough Gordon

NORTH STAR PRESS OF ST. CLOUD, INC.
St. Cloud, Minnesota

Printed in the United States of America

Published by
North Star Press of St. Cloud, Inc.
P.O. Box 451
St. Cloud, Minnesota 56302

www.northstarpress.com

Dedication

This book is dedicated to my family, Lamar, Cedar, and Mark,
without whom there would be no story to tell

Acknowledgements

It takes a village to write a book. This book's village has spread so far and for so long that it's difficult to remember every supporter.

First, we owe so much to the many friends and others who were a big part of our lives during our early sailing years, some of whom were hardly mentioned in this book. The Meredith family, that encouraged us every time we met up on the East Coast, and the Sheridan family, who gave us an outboard motor for the dinghy and supported us throughout our voyage, come especially to mind. Vera's husband Steve Dyck, barely mentioned in the book but invaluable in his confidence that no problem is fatal, supported Mark frequently in thinking through and fixing numerous mechanical problems. He even showed up along the Erie Canal to replace a starter with Mark. We are also indebted to the cheery presence of thirteen-year-old Amber Dyck, who lived with us for five days along the Erie Canal. And finally, thanks to Walkie, diesel mechanic extraordinaire, who prepared our engine for the trip, gave advice over the phone while we were out there, and empowered Mark to become his own mechanic. Without Walkie, our engine might never have left the dock.

Without lots of encouragement I might never have started writing and I certainly wouldn't have endured the eight or so drafts that evolved over the several years it has taken to bring this manuscript to fruition. In particular I want to thank two special uncles, Gil and Murray, both of whom told me to write. "You'll write a book someday," Gil told me when I was in the fifth grade. Uncle Murray said to me, "You have a book in you, but you have to figure out what you are going to say." It took awhile, but he was right. I am still figuring out what I have to say.

A special thanks to Lacey Louwagie, who gave me countless insights on how to craft an unwieldy manuscript into a coherent story, and to my editors at North Star, who are (as we speak) patiently bringing a first-time writer into her own as we learn together what was the essence of our sailing experience, and what will resonate with readers.

And to my mom, meticulous editor who catches mistakes that everyone else misses.

Last but not least, thanks to my family—Mark, Cedar, and Lamar—who have endured many a late supper and bug-eyed mom so that our story would find its way to print.

Table of Contents

Katya on Lake Huron, age nine.

Introduction

When did our thirst for watery adventures begin? When I was a teenager I found myself out on Lake Huron one day in a wind that was a tad too strong for our small vessel. We were in our eighteen-foot sailboat, *Sunlight*. Clouds scudded briskly across the sky and the wave tips sprayed us as we pounded along. My dad, chief of all family adventures and initiator of today's sail, was the captain. My sister Vera and my cousin Val were there too. I was at the bow enjoying the splashing and swaying, when suddenly the boat began to spin rapidly. The headsail, no longer flying in front of me, flapped uncertainly then did a total about-face, flattening against my body as we changed direction. I ducked, and the sail whipped past me, instantly heeling the boat over the other way.

"Dad!" I shouted in consternation, just as I saw a rotten piece of wood slide by in the green water near my dangling feet. Could it be? I scrambled to the cockpit.

My dad was, for the first time in memory, shocked into stillness. His words were short. "The rudder's gone. We're out of control."

The rudder is the critical slab of wood below and behind the boat. It attaches to the tiller, or steering device. When the tiller moves, the rudder follows, and the boat turns. To lose the rudder was nothing short of disastrous. For three silent seconds we took this information in. Then we burst into action. Vera and Val hunkered down in the center of the cockpit, low and stable. I flipped the now-useless headsail loose, crawled out on the bow, and pulled down the flapping sail. Without steerage, it would never take us where we wanted to go. The boat spun in circles and rocketed in the swells as my dad readied the tiny outboard motor for this most important job in its so-far uneventful life. The outboard sputtered to life. When the stern of the boat was underwater, the outboard valiantly pushed us toward the harbor a mile or two away. Every time the stern was thrust upward by a wave, we lost control and spun around.

Sometime in the next hour it became clear that, slow and erratic as our progress was, it *was* progress, and we would probably make it to shore without help. We arrived at the pier and zoomed willy-nilly into the protected waters behind it. The breaking waves followed us in with a roar, seemingly eager for one last shot at overturning us. Then, they flattened and it grew calm. We glanced at each other and burst into uproarious laughter, already glorying in the story we would soon be telling our family.

* * *

My husband, Mark, was a rock climber. As a young adult he climbed voraciously, setting himself goals and traveling the country in search of ever-more remote and difficult peaks to scale. Climbing satiated his thirst for living on the edge while allowing him an intimate relationship with the cliffs beneath him. Up close and dirty with the rock, he thrilled in the wee bit of control one has over an environment dominated by the merciless elements.

Mark was also a wilderness instructor for boys. He took them canoeing, backpacking and climbing. One year he had the opportunity to take them sailing on Lake Superior. He'd never been out on the water and learned along with the boys. Soon after, he witnessed Ted, captain and father he'd never met before, slide his little boat into tight spots and careen it gracefully over rough waters. Mark watched Ted's every move, awestruck, and his obsession with cliffs and vistas changed overnight into a passion for wind and waves. The setting would be different, but the elements were still up close and personal. He befriended Ted and learned all he could about harnessing the limitless energy of the wind. Soon he owned his own little boat. All his climbing gear found its way aboard and he never looked back. And then he met me.

Had I gazed into a crystal ball, I would have seen things to make me hesitant to embrace family sailing. What if I'd seen that two-hour sail that turned into a four-hour nightmare, with water spraying into the cabin through the portholes, our daughters Cedar (then three) and Lamar (less than one) sobbing and throwing up, and the engine keyhole breaking open as we tried to stick in the key—right as we headed for a rock? After that trauma, I was sick of the whole thing. *Why do we torture our children and ourselves?* I wondered. *Let's get off the water and have a normal life!*

Apparently I didn't listen to this voice because a month after that incident, in a remote corner of Lake Superior, we were motoring through narrow straits on a gray day. After six weeks on the water, we were heading home. Cedar was taking a nap in the v-berth, and Lamar was in my arms at the foot of the main hatch. Mark was in the cockpit steering. A rare break in the action of life aboard with toddlers afforded Mark and me a moment of conversation.

"So what do you think the wind will do tomorrow?" I asked, knowing that this would be a topic about which my quiet husband would have something to say. I never found out what he thought, because right then, with a loud grinding noise, the boat reared up like a bucking bronco. We all fell backwards. The boat lurched forward, then down, then lay on its side, still complaining noisily.

"Whoa! Whoa!" Mark called fruitlessly. I held Lamar tightly in one arm and turned off the engine with the other, trying to understand what just happened. I figured it out when Mark grabbed the VHF radio and called for help, his voice kept carefully low but still betrayed by a little shaking. "We are on a reef in the Moffat Straits." We were not as alone as it felt, and in minutes he made contact with the Coast Guard and nearby boaters. Help was just a few miles away.

After the comforting crackle of the radio, all was quiet. Our boat was lying on its side. There was little wind and just ripples washing gently along our hull, not quite high enough to wash in on the low side. Mark urgently searched the hull where he could see it, looking for damage. He rechecked the life raft deployment instructions. I waded through the mess in the cabin, which was lying at a fifty-degree angle, and peeked into the v-berth where Cedar was groggily waking up. I thanked God for the pillows that had cushioned her catapult to the side of the v-berth.

"Cedar, honey, you've got to get up and come out here. We hit a rock . . ."

Obediently, she came forward. "Kind of a mess in here, Mom," she commented cheerfully.

We lifted both girls out of the cabin, donned lifejackets, and sat up on the high deck. We were not far from land but the dinghy was folded and stored away. If the boat suddenly moved or sank, we would be using the life raft. The water was probably around sixty degrees. I peered in horror at the smooth rock below, just one foot underwater, knowing that a few feet away the water was thirty feet deep. Mark lifted up the floorboards. Water sloshed around in the bilge underneath. We didn't know where the water came from, but a large hole in the boat seemed likely. A tugboat was on its way. The boat lurched and we stopped breathing again.

"We hit a rock," I murmured again to Cedar. "But we're about to be rescued." My shaking voice settled as I realized the truth of this. Cedar quickly concluded that this was just another "adventure" and began snapping the clothespins along the lifelines (our equivalent of a net fence) to make Lamar laugh.

In twenty minutes we heard the distant rumble of an engine, and a tiny dinghy came into sight. It motored up to us. Two men were aboard. "Got in a bit of a pickle, eh?" I heard as rough, kind hands reached in to swing the children to safety.

Our rescuers were hardy Canadian fisher men and women. Their message to us was clear: anyone who comes to grief in this god-forsaken part of the lake is one of the family. They whisked the girls and me away to the tugboat, where anxious wives served us chips and soda and voiced outrage at the unmarked reefs in the channel. Back outside, we watched the drama unfold. The Canadians had evidently seen this kind of thing before. They expertly pulled the boat off the rock with some heavy-duty chain. She was good as gold—barely a scratch on her quarter-inch steel hull. The vent for the water tanks and the sink had poured thirty gallons of water into the cabin, soaking cushions and clothes and filling the bilge. Broken eggs and bruised egos were the extent of the damage. Our rescuers never charged us a dime.

After this near-disaster, something crystallized for Mark and me. We knew that we had made an inexcusable mistake, and come away unscathed. On the other hand, we could be vigilant and still get burned. We read of a sailing family who, through no fault of their own, got smashed in the middle of the night by a ship in the ocean. (Extreme negligence on the part of the ship's crew explained the tragedy). The boat sank in minutes, and all but the mother died.

Rescue in northern Lake Superior.

Things happen. What does one do with this reality? Anticipate and dread? Cower with shame? Shrink from any risk at whatever cost? Sometimes these things are beyond our control. Our path, we realized, was simply to give it our very best, take reasonable precautions, and move forward with both confidence and humility.

Besides, the good moments always outweighed the bad. That very evening I lounged on the cabintop with Cedar, who was shouting loudly to passing fishermen. Dark skiffs were silhouetted against a pink and gold sky. Cedar knew that fishermen were her new best friends.

"Did you catch any fish?" she hollered. One lone fisherman threw up his hands up in mock despair—not a one. She shrugged back and rolled her eyes—What can you do? Lamar tottered in the cockpit and chortled, pre-verbal but palpably delighting in the scene. Within a year she would be dogpaddling in the water to the front of the boat and shouting "Alone! Alone!" just in case I dared assist in her attempts to climb, hand-over-hand, up the anchor chain. You can't request times like these. They are blessings that come with the territory.

Our story began as one family's earnest attempt to get off the beaten path and out there into the world of adventure—to bust through our own limitations and to realize a semblance of our dreams. Many lessons came to us the hard way. Today, we feel a sense of ease as our children grow older and our voyaging style morphs into "tried and true" rather than "dive in and hope for the best." I have a sneaking suspicion that Mark's and my inclination to be together as a family and to live life with a vision is a common if not universal desire. Like everyone else, we love stories that remind us to ask for more than what's right in front of our noses.

Chapter One

Getting Started

One day soon after we'd met, Mark and I were biking along Lake Superior's northeast corner. It was as warm as it gets along the north shore. I was chatting away and Mark was listening. Abruptly he suggested we pull into a local marina, mentioning that he dreamed of sailing around the world someday. That sounded good to me, as did virtually everything he said back then. The next moment, we were gazing at a black, red, and cream-colored sailboat with real wooden masts. It was propped up unceremoniously in the parking lot, but anyone could tell it deserved better. Unbelievably, a "FOR SALE" sign was taped to its side.

"This is the kind of boat I want," Mark breathed, reverently tapping its hull.

After this brief encounter with the boat, we went about getting to know each other so that we could hook up for life. Spring turned to fall before we returned to the marina. Our dream boat was gone. Had it ever really existed? We got our answer as we spotted it sitting in someone's back yard a few miles down the road. We pulled into the driveway and met Randy, the owner. The boat was still for sale, and he liked us. He wasn't ready to sell the boat to just anyone, but he might hand it off with the loving arms of a protective father, given the right buyers and the right price.

I took a passing glance around the boat's interior—the first cabin I'd ever seen—and noted the lovely wood paneling. While I gave my trusting and ignorant approval to the interior, Mark did a thorough and complete assessment of the hull, the rigging, and the sails. We both pronounced it perfect. And Randy must have been convinced that we would treat her right.

So now we had this boat, and it was time to see what she could do. Except that, in northern Minnesota, it didn't take long before she was under two feet of snow. As spring returned and the snow began to melt, we ruefully pondered the situation. We tested the jack stands holding our boat—for the time being named *Boat*—over the ground. They were lying in deep, slippery mud. *Boat* weighed 15,000 pounds and was sinking fast.

Our first job was to get her out of the yard and back into the marina parking lot. Our second job was to get her ready for our honeymoon, in approximately two months. We planned to work on her every weekend in April before our May twelfth wedding. Two weeks before the wedding, *Boat* still sat implacably in the marina parking lot while thirty-knot winds and snow flurries whipped by. The job before us was to strip and paint the masts. We'd already painted the hull but with temperatures hovering in the forties, each coat took days to dry. I fumed, cried, and used the heat gun to warm up my hands. My heart was set on an outdoor wedding, and I was sure that it could never happen. Plus, *Boat* would never be ready on time. So much for sailing away into the sunset. Mark, silent and content, continued to scrape and paint. When I reminded him of our dire circumstances, he gave me a loving kiss. "It will all work out."

He was right, of course. We couldn't exactly sail *Boat* up to our wedding site sixty miles up the shore, but the masts were up and *Boat* was in the water by May twelfth.

We moved into the marina the day after our wedding and hung a swinging chrysanthemum off the bow to announce our new status to passersby along the marina walk. I began married life by lying prostrate on the settee with a sinus infection. At least I couldn't smell the diesel fumes that permeated the cabin. Mark smiled and kissed me again.

I was in no mood for gaiety. "I'm freezing."

Undaunted, he suggested, "Shall I install the wood stove?" Thus began our honeymoon.

Wedding on Lake Superior.

We left the dock five days and one course of antibiotics later. At first, everything went smoothly. We sailed easily up to a new marina in our low-lying two-masted ketch. Black hull, wooden masts, rust-colored sails. Compared to the average fiberglass yacht—white with blue trim, blinking with electronics—we looked like a pirate ship, fresh out of the Caribbean. People were fascinated with our traditional boat. Were we going far? Where were we from? We nodded our heads sagely and answered questions until they asked us how long we'd been out, and we were forced to admit, "Oh, about twenty-four hours."

Now, both Mark and I take pride in our outdoor prowess. We spent much of our pre-married life taking delinquent teenagers into all conditions on wilderness expeditions. We hiked many miles in woods and on snowpacked mountains, soaking wet or freezing cold. We paddled into fierce headwinds and breaking waves. We broke up fights near cliffs and ate soggy mac-and-cheese at midnight. We were confident of our ability to gear up for anything. But on this maiden voyage we fell short in two critical areas—clothing and food. We'd packed warm layers completely appropriate for cold conditions on land. What we needed—and what we vowed never to sail without again—were down coats and sailing "foulies"—thick waterproof bibs and coats suited to sitting in cold, windy weather for an indefinite number of hours.

In theory, we knew that May on Lake Superior was radically unpredictable and potentially, um, chilly. But we were caught off guard by the icy wind that kept temperatures in the cabin just above freezing. Only a quarter inch of steel and a trifling layer of foam separated us from water that was close to ice.

Likewise with food. When provisioning for the trip, I had wondered how one ate on a boat. The closest thing I knew was eating by a campfire. So I prepared to camp. I bought noodles, rice, oats, and freeze-dried beans, plus some apples for fun and a few precious hot chocolate packets. Sitting on our frozen toes in the cockpit one chilly day early in the trip, we sipped hot water. All the hot drinks were gone.

"So, why don't we have more tea?" Mark was trying not to be critical. I looked at him sheepishly and had no answer.

I was taking my first lesson in boat provisioning—a process that would have many evolutions through the years. By the time we reached a grocery store I'd figured out that weight was not an issue on a boat. Cans and unlimited hot drinks entered the scene. I learned how many uses butter has, particularly when we were chilly, working hard, and perpetually shot with adrenaline as every day we encountered moments of life-altering crisis. Our motor died as we drifted toward shore. We ran aground in muddy water. Our boat got pinned to the wrong side of the dock.

One day we found ourselves in a thick fog, but also in bright sunlight. The fog was no more than twenty feet high. Twenty-knot winds blasted through our thin layers of clothing but it was exhilarating to watch *Boat* slide easily over four- to six-foot waves.

"I've never been able to sail in these conditions before," Mark commented, equally intimidated and excited.

I nodded and grinned, shivering violently. We were crossing a thirty-mile stretch of lake and were quickly approaching a shoreline we could not see. We kept the sails full and our eyes peeled. Suddenly Mark came striding back from the bow, shouting something. Thirty feet above us a dim ray of sunlight glinted off something—glass? What could it be? Frantically I scanned ahead.

A ship—we're in the shipping lane! I thought, aghast. I pushed the tiller over hard with my numb fingers, away from the glass.

"No—other way!" Mark was in the cockpit by now. "No! Other way!" he commanded again with such authority that I swung the tiller back the other way, certain I was heading straight into death. But he had figured out that the glass was a windowpane high up on a cliff just fifty feet in front of us. We had sailed into a bay and were just feet away from shore.

We were newbies in this world of vast waters, heartless winds, heavy steel boats, and finicky engines. When our honeymoon ended and we returned to shore, I blessed the earth beneath my feet. Safe, comfortable civilization. I never wanted to leave land again. But that night, in a windless pizza restaurant, we looked at each other's red faces, wild hair, and squinty, bloodshot eyes. With a few hours' distance from our wild week together, perspective had already shifted. I had no words yet to describe the experience, but I knew I couldn't wait to tell my dad. "How was it?" I asked Mark.

"Great," he answered without hesitation.

Chapter Two

In the Family Way

*B*oat, whom we soon christened *Amicus* (Um-EE-cus), was our first new family member. *Amicus* means "friend" in Latin, and has many derivative meanings in modern languages relating to friendship and love. *Amicus* was also the name of an organization I was privileged to work for that epitomized the way we aspired to live. Amicus, Inc., was dedicated to successfully reintegrating adult and juvenile offenders to society. To us, *Amicus* meant all that was hopeful in spirit and nonjudgmental in practice. Surely, we would feel strength being sheltered and transported under such a name.

After our honeymoon, we went back to our full-time jobs and got out on the lake only when schedules allowed. Our "normal" life returned. Mark was busy hiring wilderness instructors and training them to take troubled adolescent boys canoeing. I was busy starting up a similar program for teenage girls. We were absorbed in risk management systems, cognitive theories, and circle facilitation. We ate granola bars, climbed rope courses, and packed first aid kits. Then one day, driving down the highway together, Mark opened the conversation with a quirky, vulnerable smile that meant he really cared about what he was about to ask. "So," he said, "what's the plan?"

I thought he meant the plan for the next year or so of our life, perhaps the timing of children. So I told him what was on my mind. "I want to do one big triathlon before getting pregnant."

He swept this inconsequential detail away with his hand. Clearly there was something bigger on his mind. "How about a seven-year plan?"

Seven years! Since when had I thought about anything seven years ahead?

He spoke like one who had secretly thought long and hard. The plan was simple: take five years to have two children and work hard enough that we could sell everything and live aboard *Amicus* for, say, two years. Having laid it out, he swung into a gas station. "We're out of gas."

Back on the road, I was ready with my answer. "The Plan sounds good to me."

I had never in my life said "no" to an adventure, and now that I had a husband to do all the visioning, life with kids was starting to look a lot more exciting. Mark breathed again, and we became a family with a Purpose.

That summer, I swam, biked, or ran most every day, and we made a plan that would make the most of our two-week vacation. I would swim 2.5 miles, bike 112 miles, and run 26.2 miles—an ultratriathlon. About twenty-four hours after I finished, and after a nine-hour drive, we would hop on *Amicus* with twelve good days to go.

The triathlon was a blast—everything I'd hoped for. After it, we drove to the marina and got on board. All was according to plan. The weather was squally, and the waves were bumpy. In the last twenty-four hours I had eaten several rounds of energy food—energy bars and sugar-goos—made specially for athletes and not to be confused with actual food. Distinctly un-hungry after the strenuous exercise, I nibbled grapes and crackers. I was happy, but depleted. Mark and our crew for the trip, his old friend Doug, got us out in the big waters just at dusk, heading straight for Isle Royale National Park, 150 miles away. As planned, I headed to the v-berth to sleep.

Thirty minutes later, in my exhausted stupor, I heard waves slapping the boat. I was supposed to be having the sleep of my life, and it wasn't happening. By the time I realized that the discomfort I was feeling had a name—nausea—the mere thought of what I should do (get layered up, go sit in the cockpit, prepare ginger drinks, eat protein) was beyond my capacity. Instead, I focused my mind on the plastic bags stored under the sink. Could I reach them in time?

And so it was that Mark, contentedly sailing through a squall, had just remarked to Doug, "Hmmm, I wonder how my new wife is doing?" when he heard the unmistakable sound of retching.

"Oohhhhh," he was recorded to have said, stepping down the companionway hatch into pitch blackness to find me shivering and retching uncontrollably, although I had managed to find the plastic bag in the nick of time.

"Um," he said.

"Outside," I croaked. He helped me find my foulies and brought up beef jerky at my request. I stared into the squally darkness and chewed the beef jerky. And thus I learned that everything does not always go according to plan.

* * *

By late fall, I was pregnant. Cedar arrived at the start of the following summer. Our focus shifted abruptly. The wilderness program for girls was in good hands, and I stayed home. Mark began taking time off, even though it was summer. His staff were excited about our Plan and willingly covered for him. But sailing was not going to be easy anymore. In fact, just getting to the marina was not going to be easy. It was a two-hour drive and, at six weeks, Cedar was not one of those babies who slept in a car seat. After a four-hour drive that included two stops to nurse and another for an emergency lunch break, we finally made it to the marina. The plan was to go for a day sail with our friends Matt and Patti and their infant daughter.

In the cabin, Patti and I chatted about nursing and sleep deprivation while we strapped our babies safely in their car seats before takeoff. We got out of the marina without incident—but then the engine stopped working just minutes from shore. Laughter and conversation died instantly. Mark and Matt spoke in low, terse voices as they fiddled with the engine's knobs. The babies slept peacefully. Patti and I sat and stared at each other with unmasked anxiety. Neither of us could think of a single thing to say. Thunder growled in the distance. Mark got on the radio. Rescuers motored out of the marina, their voices crackling comfortingly over the air waves. They towed us back to our dock, and we efficiently learned two things: living on the edge wasn't fun anymore, and everyone was eager to help when young children were involved.

A few weeks later we set out on our first real trip with Cedar aboard. Out on the water, she sat in a car seat in the cockpit while I sat beside her at the tiller. Soon we would toss the car seat out forever as a vehicle of misery for the baby, a waste of space for us, and an illusion, at best, of safety. But at the time, we were following advice we'd read about in sailing magazines

It was daytime and not rough, but Mark clipped himself in up at the bow. Cheerfully he adjusted sails. "How's it going?" he called back to the cockpit, certain that our newest and most precious crew member was happily absorbing the nautical vibes that would dominate her life. I could not answer him. It was effort enough to hold myself together.

The day was bright and sparkling. The wind was gusty. Each blast seemed worse than the one before it, heeling us over sideways. Before long, tears were flowing—mostly mine. I knew, theoretically, that there was not nearly enough wind to flip over *Amicus*'s 15,000-pound hull. But I was a new mom, and my hormones had no doubt that my baby was just inches from an icy death. Visions of the whole car seat careening over the side, baby trapped under those invincible straps, marched relentlessly through my mind every time I saw a dark gust coming across the water.

Without a smile, wave, or any response at all from me, Mark probably guessed that things back in the cockpit were not as they should be. He reefed (shortened) the sails to ensure that we would not be overpowered, even for a second. He hurried back to his dutiful spot at the tiller and tried to reassure me. But my tears didn't stop until we pulled into a safe harbor.

Mark slowed the boat to a virtual stop and then dashed up to the bow to grab the mooring. I pulled Cedar out of the car seat, carried her into the cabin, and nursed her until we were both dozing. We lay

Aboard *Amicus* with a new baby.

down. Mark made the boat shipshape, checked the weather forecast, got a snack, cleaned the cabin, poured himself a cup of tea, and finally sat down with a book. When I woke, I gave him a passing glance, and nursed Cedar again. "Sounds like the winds will be gusty for a few days," he remarked. I had no comment.

We sat there for three days waiting for a weather change. When it finally came, we returned to our homeport in a dead calm. This time I had Cedar in my arms. She quickly adjusted to nursing while *Amicus* was in motion. And the mother lion inside of me knew that if we were courting instant death, at least we were in it together.

As the summer wore on, and into the next summer, things improved. My fears of imminent death receded. We squeezed in three-week trips around Mark's work schedule, feeling triumphant if we made it more than one hundred miles from our homeport. We learned to embrace the slow and mundane daily rituals that accompany life with a baby. It could be tiring; it was also comforting. I came to love the ritual of washing diapers in a bucket every day. If I bent properly at the waist it was very close to yoga.

There were issues. Storms, for instance.

Now, I used to think I knew storms. I grew up taking summer backpacking trips in the Rockies of Wyoming with my dad and the college students he taught. I wouldn't see my mom for a month and chose

a college girl as a surrogate each time. It was the eighties—pre-Gortex. We wore blue jeans and flannel shirts, and we put on smelly nylon ponchos if it rained. Blisters usually covered my feet as I learned to travel at an adult pace at ten years old. More than once, I crouched under a boulder at 12,000 feet to wait out a blinding hailstorm. Then later, as a young adult, I took teenagers all over mountainous or lake-

Me and my dad, 1979.

18

filled terrain, sometimes encountering blizzards at high altitudes or jarring thunderstorms that barely gave us time to get off the water.

I didn't know all this was child's play compared to storms on big water. When we started sailing together, Mark and I developed a complex relationship with storms. Although we avoided them, we felt more confident each time we survived one. We didn't want to live on the edge, but we did want to face the elements with courage and determination. We didn't want to pretend we were as strong as the storm, but we did want to become skilled at harnessing its strength. In practice this meant that Mark vigilantly stayed on top of the forecast, avoided rough weather when possible, and proved himself calm and competent when we found ourselves in a chaotic situation. Now and then, he even cracked a wry grin in the midst of it all.

But with a baby in the cockpit, everything changed. We avoided not only storms, but also potential storms and bad forecasts in general. But even this level of prevention was not foolproof.

Once when Cedar was a year old, we made a break from our anchorage to a marina twenty miles away. Storm clouds brewed overhead, but we had a reasonable chance of making the marina before it all broke loose. We were within five miles of our destination when Cedar and I took to the v-berth for a nap. While we lay there, I heard gentle splashing sounds that hadn't been there before. A new, cool breeze wafted through the cabin. Goosebumps rose on our skin and I reached for a blanket. Mark came down and put on a lightweight raincoat. He then jacked the engine up to eighteen RPMs. This was highly unusual.

I peered out the companionway hatch. Waves were growing in front of my eyes. Mark was focused on the point we had to reach before turning in. I checked the GPS. We were over four miles from the harbor, going five knots.

"We'll get there in the nick of time," I said.

Mark didn't answer. There was no need. Within five minutes, we were down to three knots. Mark came down to change clothes again—this time into layers and foul-weather bibs.

"Can you watch outside for a minute?" he asked.

"Sure," I gulped and climbed out. Even my head felt too high. I cowered and ducked in the cockpit.

A low, black cloud swept right over us, bringing with it stinging rain and gusts up to fifty knots. Dark, angry waves spewed into the boat on both sides. When Mark returned, I jumped below. Shaking, I put on my jacket and harness. I was all prayers and swears, full of foul-weather piety. My gut comment, "Shit, shit—" turned, with an eye to my innocent baby, into the more calming phrase, "Hail Mary, Mother of Grace." I had no Catholic background and didn't know what I was saying, but I hoped God would not get petty at a time like this. It was all I could think of under the circumstances.

Standing in the companionway hatch, I watched Mark and the waves and the weather behind him. He was wet and wind-whipped. I was dry and protected, though only four feet away. We were together, though we spoke little. "There's no lightning, is there?" I offered. Every time I peeked at the oncoming waves and weather, I was afraid I would pee in my pants. So I stopped looking.

Without speaking, Mark turned the boat 180 degrees. As we swooped around, water poured onto the decks. We went downwind for a few seconds. I thought we might be turning back. But a few seconds later, Mark turned again, broadside to the waves for a harrowing second, then back into the wind. We slowed to a near stop, but Mark kept going. He did another 360, and his face relaxed just a hair. "Once this cloud passes over us, I think it's going to mellow," he said.

I breathed deep and willed my shoulders to fall. I thought, *I don't know a single mother who would do this with her baby.*

Just then, Cedar woke up, and I jumped to the front of the cabin. The v-berth lifted her into a sitting position, then dive-bombed back down. On the next pitch, she plummeted straight into my arms. I stood there, jammed against the bulkhead, watching the water slosh around outside the portholes, just inches away. As soon as I could move, we staggered to the settee. With a crackling voice, I sang a few songs, keeping an eye on Mark. I could feel the chop rising again.

After a while, Cedar moved just enough to indicate that she wanted to nurse. I peeled off my layers, and sat with her for another long while. Mark's face was looking good. The worry lines were smoothing out. "I can see the town!" he called.

I gave him a thumbs-up. Each foot we traveled brought us deeper into a protected bay. It was a good thing too. The skies were darkening again, this time with flashes of lightning. "I'm going to need help when we get into the marina," he called.

"Just give me a thirty-second warning," I answered. A few minutes later, we swung dramatically around. Suddenly, the waves were gone. We were in the channel. Thunder started to crash around us. We radioed the marina several times but could not raise a soul.

"We're aground," Mark said calmly. I looked helplessly into the marina a hundred feet away, where dozens of boats sat placidly. I sat Cedar at the bottom of the steps to watch us and get rained on, and gunned the engine in reverse while Mark hung out on the main boom. No luck. I held wet, crying Cedar below while Mark let down the dinghy to row an anchor out. Once the dinghy was floating, we lifted

Getting a breath of air in a brisk wind.

21

off and began to drift. Mark whipped the dinghy back up and motored in. "I'll go into the gas dock," he decided.

I set Cedar on the settee with an open bag of animal crackers. This unlimited gold mine shocked her into silence, then contentment. She was happy, and I was free to jump to the dock. Mark managed to turn the boat on a dime and come around perfectly in a narrow harbor with wind and rain and lightning and dark all pouring down at once. One lonely soul in an orange raincoat saw us and came out to help us swing in.

* * *

When people ask, "How do you keep Cedar safe? What do you do about storms?" I think of the highway. Most children are inches away from potential death while riding past a semi on the highway, but we take precautions, follow them without fail, and then get used to it. Was this any different? In general, our only bragging rights regarding storms lay in our ability to avoid them. We've seen enough to be humbled.

I can't help but think of the Biblical story about the disciples enduring a great storm in a tiny boat. As their frail craft faltered, they glimpsed Jesus calling from afar, and Peter, one of the disciples, leaped out of the boat to reach him. He started to sink, focused with despairing intensity on his Lord, and rose again.

When I experience the absolute terror of the sea, I think of Peter. The danger itself is usually less than the terror of our imaginations, or the possibility of acting foolishly. We have never courted instant death in a storm, but we have felt ourselves to be the tiny, helpless, inconsequential individuals that inhabit this earth, overpowered by forces beyond our control. When a storm threatens, I have come to expect a visceral survival anxiety. When I feel the fear rising, I whisper a phrase that I discovered is the most common message from angels in the Bible: "Do not be afraid." They must tell us this for a reason. What if we perish in a storm? Or what if Mark is swept overboard? While I know intellectually that the chances of tragedy are slim if we keep our wits about us and use good judgment, the possibility remains, and my gut knows this intimately. When I was twenty, my brother Danny was eighteen. He died from a fall on a backpacking trip. So I know the realities of heartbreaking, irreplaceable loss. But I'm also convinced that there is a benevolent God out there. Perhaps it is this faith in the Divine flow of Providence, continually bending even terrible events to bring good out of them (including an astonishing number of good things that came from my brother's death) that keeps me comfortable, even happy living perpetually with a certain level of risk.

"Amazing Grace," a ballad that resonates with millions around the world, was written after a storm at sea. The composer, John Newton, was a British sailor involved in the slave trade, and he was certain he was going to die. Surviving the storm proved his turning point, compelling him to eventually leave the slave trade and become a minister. I have no doubt that Providence was at work in the details of Newton's life, creating a new purpose out of a terrifying experience. Storms on mighty bodies of water do change lives. For better or worse, sailing seemed to be the thing we were meant to do. And sailing meant storms.

* * *

Sailing also meant crises, big and small. Once after a long, rolling day, coming into a marina at dusk with a current pushing us sideways, I was exhausted, woozy, and extremely focused on steering us into the narrow entrance without crashing into anything or getting swept right by. Cedar eyed a large statue and asked her hundredth question in that minute: "Is that a real moose or a pretend moose, Mommy?"

I hollered, "Shut up, Cedar! I mean be quiet, please!"

She quieted down, we came successfully into our dock, and I vowed never again to judge a mother yelling at her child in moments of stress. I eyed Cedar guiltily, but she had already forgotten and was on to the next question. When would I remember? Moral outrage means nothing to humans under seven years old.

Mark was calmer in crisis—at least on the outside. Once as we crossed a very shallow section, he leaned over the bow, his eyes glued to the water. I was steering. Cedar announced she needed to poop. She'd recently graduated from the child's potty in the cockpit to an elevated composting toilet inside the cabin, which she couldn't use alone.

"Can't you wait?" I was impatient, while Mark's true worth as a father surfaced. Estimating that we had at least two minutes before the

Storytime.

water got dangerously shallow, he instructed me to shift to neutral, swung Cedar into his arms, and hopped down. Soon the deed was done.

One evening I was preparing a meal that was fast and filling—corned beef hash with fried eggs. Suddenly a fire burst out, right in the stove.

"Mark!" I shouted with urgency, before thinking about the fire extinguisher.

Mark appeared instantly, but displayed no panic. "It's not a real fire," he assured me.

"It looks pretty real to me!" I retorted. He put a calming hand on my back. The girls came to watch. In a few seconds, the alcohol had burned up and the fire disappeared.

The next year, we bought a propane stove. This time, when I saw flames, I remembered. I calmly called Mark, as a precaution. He instantly grabbed the fire extinguisher off the wall and detonated the entire area.

"Dinner is ruined," I said stupidly.

"Yeah, but the boat's saved," Mark pointed out. Apparently that fire was real. To me, fire is fire; his explanation of the difference between propane and alcohol stoves went mostly over my head. But that was all right. Between us, we covered most of the bases.

While Mark worked on our systems, I figured out how to nurse on a boat. Cedar wanted to nurse whenever she needed to fall asleep or when she was seasick or bored, which was, let's face it, much of her waking time. I resisted this. "I will only nurse every two hours," I decided. But when I got seasick, I could hardly lift my head. Cedar, on the other hand, became hyper, naughty, and slightly hysterical. This was not a good combination. All the advice I'd heard on seasickness (drink lots, sleep whenever possible, watch the horizon, take drugs) helped me to manage my seasickness when I could do them. But they never worked for Cedar. And, as any parent knows, the likelihood of either one of us being able to take a nap on demand was about as likely as a child gobbling up a new curry recipe—it might happen once, under a miraculous combination of circumstances, but should never be expected as the norm. Nursing, on the other hand, was instantly available under almost any circumstances. Most important, it soothed us both.

One morning when we were both feeling queasy, Cedar and I took to the v-berth. She nursed, and dozed, then nursed some more. I decided to see how long this could go on. I waited, then dozed off. We lay together for almost three hours. When she finally broke free, she was relaxed, happy, and chortling. So was I. Instead of being annoyed that she was so needy, I felt grateful that the milk machine offered such a ready antidote to seasickness, weariness, and other stressors on her small body.

One stressor that all but disappeared on the boat was separation anxiety. While on board, Cedar demonstrated no anxiety about not being close enough to us. She didn't need to worry about us because we were always within ten feet of her. Instead of following us around, calling for us, or crying if we weren't close enough, she simply got on with the important business of growing brain cells and refining her motor coordination. We were temporarily freed from the questions of, "Can our child handle a babysitter, or daycare, or sleeping alone?" As a mom who overintellectualized this issue and had plenty of separation anxiety on land, I loved this reprieve. I could simply be with my child and not have to strive toward an optimal amount of togetherness or separateness. And for Mark, being around his daughter all the time, feeling her love and comfort with him grow exponentially with their time together, was all the reward he needed.

Chapter Three

Around Lake Superior

T he following fall, Lamar was born. How obliging of her to come in September! She had the winter and spring to prepare for her first trip—a 1,200-mile circumnavigation of Lake Superior. It was our shakedown for bigger things. We knew it would be a lot of work, but heck—living on land with a toddler and a baby is a lot of work too. We might as well be tied to the boat as to our living room.

When we took off, Lamar was nine months old and eagerly taking her first steps. Cedar, at three, had a developmentally appropriate but wildly inconvenient goal—to push as many buttons as physically possible every hour. While Lamar was still tied to us, more or less, with a harness or cloth baby carrier, Cedar skipped away the minute our backs were turned and headed for the depth sounder, the GPS, the pretty red lights on the engine controls. "CEDAR!" was Mark's and my password to each other to cause interference ASAP, and Cedar's clue to jump out of reach.

Our trip around Lake Superior granted us lots of practice coming into unfamiliar anchorages. Having made many lifestyle choices that the average North American might look askance at, such as birthing our babies in the living room, or foregoing vaccinations, I decided that dropping an anchor was like practicing a lifestyle choice. The more proactive we were about it, the harder the effort initially appeared, but the happier we felt in the end. It could be easy to take the path of least resistance—to go to the known anchorages, to assume that a holding was doing what it was supposed to do, to consider the anchorage apart from the land masses surrounding it or the weather that would engulf it.

Lamar learns to walk.

Mark, always wary of the easy way out, had a different philosophy: "Question it now so you don't have to question it later." His days could be full of excitement, but at night he preferred to sleep. Dubious protection from predicted winds, potential bouncing in swells, or sketchy bottoms that might not hold the anchor were all reasons to move.

Sometimes we observed other crews coming in. We watched the quick-and-temporary style, the cautious-and-vigilant style, and the fraught-with-complications style. We didn't have anything over anybody. Coming into an anchorage was rarely a smooth event for us. Once as the swell dropped and as unfamiliar, lethal landmasses approached, the girls and I emerged from the cabin, still a bit seasick but also starving. On the bowsprit Mark, with his Buddhist leanings, breathed deeply. He projected without sounding angry.

"Over here!" he called.

He faithfully gave me the hand motions to confirm his words. I held the tiller in one hand and Lamar in the other, anxiously scanning the scene. I could feel my pulse increase and my voice get sharp as I shifted into neutral and watched our speed drop. In a best-case scenario, both girls would be harnessed in at this point, free to watch from the bow. But Cedar had refused to wear hers or to go below, and I was too preoccupied to give this insubordination the attention it deserved. So she sat in the cockpit. I arched my neck, craning to hear and see Mark on the bowsprit as he looked for a good spot and directed me with his arms. I asked Cedar to pull out the depth sounder. She bounced into the hatch, unhooked the depth sounder, carefully positioned it—and then planted herself right in front of it so I couldn't read a thing.

"Cedar!" I cried.

She shouted out random numbers to Daddy: "Ten! Five! Eight!" I pushed her out of the way.

Of more concern was the weather. I pushed her out of the way and yelled out a few numbers before she could block my vision again. Meanwhile, Lamar was wriggling and anxious to start her toddler life again, having put it on hold for hours while we lay prostrate in the cabin. Somehow, somewhere, Mark dropped the hook. "Back down!" he called, and I put us in reverse.

As we pulled back on the anchor, the water swirled around us. Cedar leaned over the lifelines, watching. "We're not moving, Mom!" she pointed out, peering intently at the shoreline. In minutes, the motor was off and all was peaceful, at least on the outside. Inside my churning heart, recovery took longer.

Half an hour later, after setting out two anchors, we cringed when another boat appeared. We were in a small lagoon, with minimal room for two. But we needn't have worried. The crew smoothly anchored a safe distance away and the skipper—who by now we could see was a father of three young children—immediately donned a wetsuit, jumped into the frigid waters, and checked not only his anchor but ours. He swam over to us to let us know that we were looking good twenty feet down. "Hey, thanks!" I called, lost in admiration.

That night Mark and I discussed our parenting-while-anchoring techniques. "We could do better," we agreed. But how? It wasn't hard to figure it out, once we put some thought to it. First, a ready snack when we neared land to keep our bodies functional in stress. Second, a promise of a "treat" at the end of a problem-free anchoring. A dried apricot on a toothpick (our version of a lollipop) was the current favorite. We informed Cedar of the new plan. She was indifferent, as this was irrelevant to the next ten minutes of her life.

The next time the motor went on and land loomed close, I was ready. Mark had his Powerbar, Lamar was just nursed, and Cedar and I were downing a bowl of rice and almonds, along with plenty of water. We headed outside. "Remember about that lollipop," I said to Cedar as we headed into the cockpit.

"I know, Mom!" Cedar planted herself in an out-of-the-way corner of the cockpit with her dolly and tea set, and was unperturbed even when an unexpected 360 turn swept the tiller through her tea party.

Chasing toddlers and anchoring without meltdowns was actually the least of our worries. More concerning was the weather,

Pukaskwa Provincial Park, Ontario.

which kept us pinned to each dock or anchorage for an average of three days while major westerly winds blew.

One morning after a three-day wait, we motored out of the sheltered anchorage and found ourselves in a predictably big swell and ten to twenty knots of wind from shifting directions. Our destination was only ten miles away, but by the time we were halfway there, the winds were on the nose—coming right at us—and the swells were huge. Storms threatened. Down below where I was with the girls, the motion was rough and unpredictable. I had taken ginger tea as a single, customary precaution against seasickness and then, when I felt the queasiness roll in, decided it had failed. Soon I was too debilitated to manage the concerted and balanced action required to dress us appropriately, harness us together, propel us out to the cockpit to find a spot to stay out of Mark's way, attach ourselves to the boat, and (finally) lock our eyes on the horizon.

Mark was too busy sailing to help until it was too late. He peeked inside the cabin just in time to see me thrust a cloth diaper under Lamar's face. She started throwing up. This was too much for me and soon I, too, was retching—on top of her, on top of the diaper, on top of my own harness and clothes. I could barely look up to say, "Thanks," as Mark scrambled around for the pile of cloth diapers, which he threw in my general direction before dashing out to take the tiller, as none of our automatic steering devices were currently functional.

Her stomach miraculously intact for the moment, Cedar cried, "I hate waves! I hate sailing!" Silently, I agreed with her.

Making no headway, Mark turned us around. I was too disheartened to comment. In a couple hours, we blew back into the anchorage we'd left. Once the anchor was safely buried, Mark came down the hatch and threw his cap on the floor, dropping onto the settee. He held his head in his hands. I cried, shook, and told my babies how sorry I was. They were uninterested. Lamar had fallen asleep the instant the motion ceased.

"Daddy, that was a rough ride!" Cedar commented cheerfully.

He could barely nod.

A few minutes later, my dampened spirits reached a breaking point, and I began to vent. We'd read so many lovely stories about sailing and kids in sailing magazines, or books written by families that circled the globe. The picture we'd created was of children, mature beyond their years, taking night watches, or diving overboard amid glorious sunsets, or absorbing world cultures. Where were the stories that matched *our* experiences? What happened to the glorious side of family sailing?

"I'd like to talk to whoever said that babies never get seasick," I threatened. "And what about babies in car seats in the cockpit?" If there was a way for them to be more seasick than they were today, that would be it. "Sleeping in a net? Since when do either of our girls sleep without someone else nearby?"

Mark, I guessed, was inwardly certain there were answers here, but for once he had no far-reaching perspective. He only hung his head.

Until that moment, we'd felt we were having a great time—or at least we assumed we should be—because we were following our dream to sail around Lake Superior. The difficulties—the constant vigilance and absence of down time, interrupted sleeping schedules and fatigue, living on top of each other, and the importance of constant watchfulness of weather to keep us safe—were subtle and took weeks to fully impact us.

On the rougher sailing days, Mark could really have used a hand, and I could really have used a break. Right when we were both maxed out, we were unavailable to each other. The frequency of overwhelming times, which were rare during our predictable life on land, sobered and confused us. Was our sailing enthusiasm foolish, our trust in this dream unrealistic? Why would we choose a lifestyle that encompassed such a wide range of miseries?

After a while I got up and peeked into the icebox. My stomach was beyond empty, which was a good indicator for the rest of the family. A yogurt container had opened up, and a thin skim of yogurt mixed with the melted ice at the bottom. Vegetables had slid into the mess. I pulled out the celery, washed it off, and found the peanut butter. Mark, tired but resolute, restacked books, wiped away vomit remains, and stored foul-weather gear.

Cedar commented, "We're back in the same place, aren't we, Mom? Do I still get an anchoring treat?" She planted herself happily on the top of the cabin hatch steps where she was at eye-level with the tuna I was mashing up with mayonnaise.

Releasing anger and disappointment was a great relief. We could stop thinking about what we *should* be experiencing, and simply live with what was really going on. Defeat and humiliation generally provide an excellent foundation for soul- and life-searching questions.

For starters, we had set ourselves an ambitious goal. Without a lot of previous experience, we were attempting to sail some of the coldest fresh waters on the planet in a slow sailboat with two toddlers. No one told us this would be easy. Few who knew Lake Superior well even thought our plan was sane—though everyone wanted to hear about it. Clearly, if we were expecting quick rewards, we would have to rethink.

So we did. First, we recalled the larger perspective that had gotten us where we were. We wanted our daughters to grow up sailing, comfortable with small spaces, nautical motion, and a simple life. We knew we'd rather endure discomfort or even fleeting despair than live on twelve-hour workdays and wait for weekends to be together. This shakedown trip was about preparation for the future, and necessitated some endurance and faith on our part.

But it wasn't all about the future, either. A few realizations were startling. "You know," Mark remarked to me, "the girls are having a great time."

When I thought about it, he was right. Far from being traumatized, they enjoyed pretty much everything. For Lamar, as long as her family was right there, all was well. There was never a dull moment, or a lack of stimulus. She loved nothing more than to nurse while I steered, her feet resting on the tiller as it moved back and forth comfortingly. Cedar's repertoire of self-devised entertainment was constantly expanding, amusing both herself and her sister.

She frequently popped her head out of the hatch and shouted "We're coming about!" ("I hope not," countered Mark.) One day, Cedar and Mark studied the charts while he explained everything she wanted to know about where we were and where we were going. Soon after, she began explaining to her dollies where they were going, and *their* last thunderstorm. Both girls often followed me around the cabin when they wanted to "help" and then took off on their own pursuits.

Cedar reminded me, if I made light of her responsibilities, that her jobs were every bit as serious as mine. We might want to go to shore, but her dollies were just about ready for a diaper change. Or she was in the middle of a chapter. Or she was still packing for her trip. Her social instincts dictated to her an intricate weave of real and imaginary relationships known to us through her monologues, often held at length on her cardboard cell phone that morphed into a handheld radio after a few weeks. "Tulip! Hello, Tulip! Wait—the coverage isn't good—okay let's try again. How *are* you? We are great, great . . . just had a rough northwest wind, but it's looking better and

Cedar plays cards in the cabin.

the forecast is sounding good so we should be outta here soon . . . yep, I'd like a hot dog and catsup. And make it snappy please. How much is the hot chocolate?"

* * *

Cedar's coming-of-age safety lessons came not from lighting a match or dashing across a busy road, but their impact was similar. One day we were sailing downwind, and Mark was slowly bringing the boom across the hatch opening and cockpit. This is an important maneuver in jybing that must be done with great care. At the moment the boom came across the hatch opening, Cedar poked her head out of the hatch. *Crack!* The boom clocked her in the head, and she skittered over to the side. "Ackk," I cried, rushing to her. She looked at me, a little startled. "I'm fine, Mom."

Mark, with his usual caution, had let the boom out very slowly. The lesson was already learned, but I couldn't help myself. "Always, always check before coming out of the cabin!" I continued. Cedar looked at me. Hadn't she just learned that lesson, better than I could ever have taught it?

Yes, Mark and I finally acknowledged, the kids might be our greatest challenge, but without them, what would be the point? Our difficulties were pushing us to be better partners and better parents. So, maybe we weren't the saltiest sailors on the block. That was okay. We weren't ready to give up. We'd face each day with a combination of effort and letting go. A few days later, after enviously watching other gnarly sailors take off into the open water in conditions we couldn't handle, we reminded ourselves that our girls were the reason we were doing this trip. We had tested the edge and knew it was there. Our decisions and actions had a strong foundation, and though they might not be glamorous, they were getting us where we needed to go. Slowly.

So, after that miserable morning, we slid into a groove, feeling a new rhythm in our daily life. Meals, which before had involved concentrated effort to prepare and clean up, and plenty of deep breathing

A good sailing day relaxing in the cockpit.

to complete without losing tempers and spilling food, began to flow like the waves under the boat, uncounted and imperceptible. I learned to use the icebox more efficiently—for short-term storage of dairy products encased in hard plastic. Vegetables went into lockers, and fruit was stored in a net above. When they ran out, we went without. I learned that I could cook our favorite meals without onions, peppers, or cheese, and nobody starved. If one orange was all that was left, the girls got to split it. They savored each section noisily while I watched, mouth watering. Cedar generously put a section in front of me. "That's for you, Mom."

Once, desperate for vegetables, I ventured into unheard of territory: I bought canned bean sprouts and canned chard. Could it satisfy our nutritional cravings for dark, leafy greens? The chard helped—in tiny doses and large one-pot meals. The bean sprouts were so un-sprouty that the second can sat in the bilge and got pulled out when we arrived home. Sometimes if you can't have the real thing, there is no substitute.

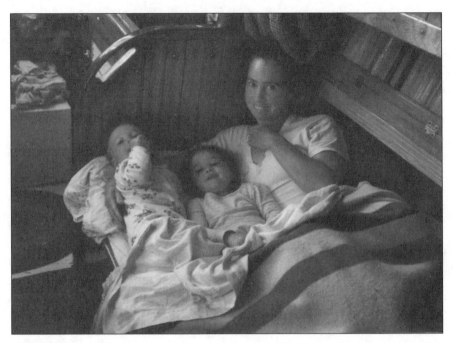

Cuddling.

We started managing extras like haircuts, cookie-baking, and finger painting. The days began to march seamlessly along, and we became aware that this trip would not last forever.

One day, as we were sailing along in a gentle breeze, Cedar was eating lunch and Lamar was playing with Mark, both in the cockpit. I was putting together a bean burrito for Mark. The wind piped up from somewhere, and we lurched over in a gust. Food, girls, and all loose items went sliding. Automatically, all four of us took quick action. In seconds, Cedar was inside on the settee with her lunch, Lamar was in my arms, all food was either gone or stable, and Mark was alone outside, adjusting the sails. And we carried on without a word.

One night, Mark set out in the dinghy to attach a line off our stern to the shore—a precaution to keep our boat from swinging aground if the wind changed direction. Cooking dinner inside, I was vaguely aware of Cedar in the cockpit yelling to Mark, "Should I throw the line? Daddy! Should I throw the line?"

He called back, "Nope—we're good!"

Cedar eventually stopped shouting and I stopped thinking about it. Later that evening, as I washed diapers in the cockpit, I noticed there was no line I could see off the stern. I asked Mark, "Where did you attach the stern line, anyway?"

Mark leaned over to check, and could not find it either. Apparently Cedar had tossed it overboard. With a crinkly and slightly chagrined smile Mark rowed to shore and fished the line out of the water while I tried to explain to Cedar what she had done wrong. She obediently dictated back to me, "Never, ever throw the line in the water!" while grinning from ear to ear, perfectly aware that we throw lines all the time. Helping was way too fun to be curtailed by foolish mantras.

Lamar was less involved in mischief-making. She was too busy observing. Peering through the netting, she watched the changing scenery. One night might bring caribou swimming across the water, another an amber sunset casting deepening shadows on our home and surroundings until all was gray and chilly. The roll and sweep of each wave mesmerized her. Occasionally, humans nearby provided entertainment—a teenage couple lying face-down on the dock, watching fish through a hole, or a team of bagpipers giving us a concert from the bow of their sailboat. Lamar didn't want to miss any of it.

Near the end of our trip, we headed for Grand Marais, Minnesota—our return to civilization after weeks in pristine woodsy anchorages. The forecast was ideal, the waves were minimal, and both girls napped on cue inside the cabin. I brought a hat and sunglasses into the cockpit, prepared for the perfect sail. Within ten minutes, the wind had died to nothing. *Amicus* glided to a standstill.

"Foiled again!" I commented.

Mark grunted. But it was a gorgeous August day, and we were feeling optimistic. We sat and waited. Within half an hour, a puff of wind appeared from behind us. Mark put up the spinnaker (light air headsail) and all the canvas that would fit—four sails in all—and we

Anchored in the wilderness.

ghosted along at a gentle two-to-three knots. We arrived in Grand Marais by late afternoon. Windblown, patched, stained, and mismatched, Cedar blew into the public library. In a distinctly non-inside voice, she exclaimed, "Mom! Dad! Look at all the *books*!" (Our books had been read to tatters.) Three neatly put-together girls were coloring at a table, and Cedar sat down amongst them. "Where are you from?" She smiled her winning smile.

The girls answered with shocked silence. One of them gave her a crayon. She blasted through a drawing, tossed it in my direction, and headed back outside.

Our trip ended in the Apostle Islands, the most popular cruising area on Lake Superior. White sails dotted the horizon. Our delight at seeing so much humanity lessened as we tried to squeeze into the only safe anchorage amongst fifty other boats. But despite the crowds, our black hull and brown masts stood out, and several sailors we'd met along our journey invited themselves aboard to see how we'd fared. Guests!

The girls were beside themselves with excitement. Lounging in the cockpit, our visitors dreamt aloud of the Caribbean and discussed their college-aged children, their electronics, and the last big blow they'd weathered. We, on the other hand, tried to keep Lamar from chowing down on all the gourmet goat cheese offered up by our guests, argued with Cedar about what liquid she was allowed to have in her plastic wine glass, and inwardly bemoaned the fact that neither girl had slept all afternoon. But it was great to have company.

On our last day, the winds were shockingly cooperative. The day's sail went smoothly until we arrived at our final destination, a marina with a tricky entrance into which we maneuvered expertly despite the sun sinking directly into our eyes.

"Hey!" A man ran up to the end of the dock we were approaching. I was at the tiller, just beginning to breathe easy. Cedar and Lamar were with me in the cockpit, rapidly reaching the end of their patience. After talking to the man who had greeted us, Mark turned to me and motioned that we would have to go to the slip two docks down.

I sighed—did this man have any idea what he was asking? As I threw the engine into reverse, Cedar cried, "Do I get my treat yet, Mom?"

Lamar let out a howl of urgency and bonked her head on the mizzen boom that never fails to catch an unsuspecting forehead in a tense moment. I gripped her and threw the engine and tiller back and forth, blindly following Mark's calm directives from the bow. After three or four attempts to back up and turn forward, he judged it would now be possible to enter the correct slip. The sun dipped below the horizon, improving our vision. I edged into the slip as slowly as I dared without losing steerage. The bowsprit was too close—it was going to hit the dock. *Crunch*. Mark jumped out and shoved it off; a little paint gone was the only damage.

It was an appropriately messy ending to our three-month journey. *Amicus* calmly nuzzled up to the dock and the engine was turned off. Silence. After tying up to the dock, Mark and I sat in a daze for about thirty seconds, which was all the time we had before the girls hopped onto the dock and ran up to explore new territory.

Two questions waited patiently in the recesses of our minds as we adjusted back to cars and car seats, grocery stores, bedrooms, work schedules, and outside responsibilities: What did we think of our trip? Would we be ready to do it, and more, again?

Seasoned crew.

Chapter Four

Leaving the Dock

S o, what do you think now about moving aboard?" Mark asked me, wearing that sweet, shy smile that portrayed vulnerability. He kept his tone casual, which didn't fool me at all. We needed to make some decisions. It was autumn, and the beautiful red maple outside our home was in its full glory. We'd been home for six weeks. He was gone all day at work, and I was at home with the girls. As many of our life-altering conversations went, this one was short.

"When did we say we were going to leave?"

"In two years, a little less." Mark let this hang in the air as if there was reason to rethink.

I pondered. Finally, I answered, "That sounds like a long time. Why were we going to wait that long?"

"Well, to earn more money, and to let the kids grow older." I considered this. It wasn't like we were stockpiling our savings in large quantities. We had read nothing to convince us that kids who were three and five would be that much easier than two and four. Besides, these were their formative years. Whether or not they remembered the trip was less important to us than how it would shape their realities. Finally, we were still basking in the sense of accomplishment from our circumnavigation of Lake Superior. Why lose all that momentum?

So I said what I thought. "Nine months sounds much better."

"Sounds good to me."

Seven months later, we sold our home, and Mark left his job. We moved into a tiny house near where *Amicus* was waiting out the winter. Her engine was being refurbished by Walkie, a legendary diesel mechanic. There, Mark embarked on a grueling regime in the bowels of the hull—grimy, upside-down, finger-pinching, toxic-fuming work. The hull needed grinding and painting, the rigging needed to be replaced, and he needed to buy, finish, and install a new mast. And those were just some of the biggies. Meanwhile, the girls and I lived a life of leisure. Lamar was nineteen months old and Cedar was almost four.

At night we discussed small spaces. If I wanted a deeper mixing bowl, Mark's job was to figure out a place where it would fit. The girls got into the act. Each of them could bring three dollies. Cedar spent hours choosing and replacing. Each dolly was unique—how to choose? She eventually selected a family that included six dollies. She assigned three of them to Lamar, who obligingly agreed.

Lamar was obliging in many ways. I was determined to lessen our dependence on diapers by departure time, and I gave her sippy cup after sippy cup of water to drink. She downed it all, and then sat on the toddler potty for long periods while we waited for the moment of truth. Cedar pitched in too; she sat beside Lamar and "read" books aloud. Before long, Lamar was using the potty on her own, to Cedar's great pride and my relief. By the time we moved aboard she wore diapers only at night, and washings in the bucket ceased to dominate the daily chores.

Naptime was another preparatory time for me. Every afternoon I secretly winnowed out undesirable playthings. Each girl was allowed to fill one cloth bag with toys. The bags would hang on the wall in the v-berth. Cedar was quite sensible; her cloth bag contained her cardboard violin and bow, her cardboard phone/radio, lots of yarn, a few rocks, and several plastic trinkets. I discretely tossed the rocks and brought out the trinkets for reconsideration. "Do you really want these? What for?" She tossed all but two. "This one is actually a bottle for my baby, and this one is food." I capitulated.

There was a third cloth bag, which would be the shared one. Since the girls played together and shared most everything, I thought this was a great idea. Cedar was scornful. "If it's not mine, I don't want it." So I filled the bag myself, with more standard items—games and puzzles, mostly. (Every now and then during our trip, in a dull moment, I pulled out something from this third bag. The girls played disinterestedly with it for a few minutes before returning to their regular lives.)

I was mulling over my things too. How could we make the spices more accessible? Would the new wok fit on the stove—and in its compartment? How would we hang pictures? How many cookbooks could I do without?

I bought dry goods in bulk and packaged them up. We filled the bilge with cans, condiments, an indefinite number of kid treats, and Ziploc bags of grains, legumes, nuts, and seeds. As non-drinkers, we didn't have to worry about alcohol. Other than emergency rations of Ramen and mac-and-cheese, I bought very little pre-packaged or ready-made food, planning to stick to the diet we'd established the summer before. I was already making all the family bread, beans, soups, and yogurt.

It felt impossible to predict what we would need for clothing. I filled a few bags with extras and stuck it in the bilge. (We would promptly forget about this until we came across it accidentally a year later.) I brought three bathing suits per girl, which turned out about right. I correctly figured that we wouldn't be changing clothes very often.

Eventually, Mark began to report milestones. He was putting things together instead of taking them apart. The new mast was upright. The rigging was half done. The SSB radio was installed, and he'd heard a forecast for the north Atlantic. That night he came home with a dreamy smile on his face. "Winds out of the northeast today— a typical tradewind day," he informed me. We were good as there! Every night we relentlessly ticked items off our lists. Mark went to the boat at 6:00 a.m. every day and pounded away until he ran out of something or it got too dark to see.

To-do lists were an inevitable part of our departure preparations. They could be overwhelming enough to stop would-be sailors in their tracks. We needed the ability to distinguish between the "must-do-before-we-leave" list (generally including only those things that were essential to the integrity of the hull and rigging), the "do-sometime" list, and the "don't-let-this-one-slide-for-months-even-though-it-means-nothing-to-you-because-it-is-very-important-to-your-wife" list. Mark was too eager to leave to expect perfection, and he was diligent about the latter list, which is one reason we are still sailing together.

In our final week on land, we felt ourselves being swept down the rapids toward departure, no longer merely in the current of preparation. One car went into storage, *Amicus* went into the water, and the list of "dones" was larger than the list of "to-dos."

One day we dutifully brought a dozen boxes below, emptied them of their contents, and returned to the dock. By the time we were finished, it was late. Why get in a car and drive home? We were already home! "Time to go to bed!" I told the girls cheerfully.

It was our first night aboard in nine months. Nine months is a long time in the life of a baby or toddler. As far as Cedar was concerned, this was all new again. Lamar had no noticeable recollection at all. We read books in the v-berth under the new little reading lights Daddy had installed. Cedar played with the lights. Lamar rolled around and laughed. I turned out the light.

"Hey, where are we?" Cedar protested. I lay down between them. The plan was for them to share the v-berth, which was what we'd done the previous summer, sort of. (Like many families, we were prone to musical beds.) They'd slept together ever since, at least for the first few hours each night. I prayed and sang, and soon their breathing sounded soft and regular. Triumph! I slid myself out. Mark had already converted the port settee to our twin-size berth, and we crawled right in. Without moving elbows, we could both read in bed.

Before he turned off the headlamp that was lighting both our books, the problems started. It was June on Lake Superior. The mosquitoes were out. We had mosquito netting over all the openings, but a few always got in. Mosquitoes were particularly attracted to Cedar. Soon the unmistakable sound of slapping echoed through the cabin.

"Mom, I'm getting bit!" She was miserable, but only half-awake, and soon drifted off.

The v-berth was so dark you couldn't see a hand in front of your face. It was great for sleeping, but only if you knew where you were. In the wee hours I heard rolling and shuffling, followed by, "Mom!" I considered. Answering was a gamble. If Cedar was almost asleep, a response might wake her up. But her shuffling didn't sound drowsy.

"Yeah, honey?" I called softly.

"I need to go potty."

Ah, well. Mark was up instantly, being on the outside of the bunk. He coaxed Cedar down to the foot of her berth where she slid into his arms. I heard the door to the tiny bathroom open. Our composting toilet was three feet off the ground to make room for the composter. In a few weeks Cedar would learn to climb up there. But tonight and for many nights after, Mark lifted her up and held her there in the dark. Before they were done, I heard another voice. "Mama?"

I sighed. It would be a long night. I brought Lamar down with me, and Mark joined Cedar in the v-berth. No berth in our cabin had room for three.

Getting ready to move aboard.

Well-wishers and friends have occasionally marveled at our ability to sell everything, move aboard, and simply sail away. One friend asked politely, "I hate to bring this up, but what will you do if you don't like it?"

But cutting ties felt neither outrageous nor courageous to me. It felt exciting and easy. I had taken it for granted when Mark and I met that we were going to live an exciting life, and we did not feel particularly attached to any place or house. I had very few close friends where we lived at the time. Those who knew us well cheered us on; if they had reservations, they kept quiet.

Going on adventures had always been a part of my life. Backpacking trips as a child led seamlessly into canoe trips as a young adult. In my family, the adventurous spirit was heralded as a virtue— the more remote the destination, the better. My parents were eager that we lived lives that were full and meaningful. They were not as focused on bringing in money. They recognized that these two things did not always go together. Most importantly, my parents were not worriers. My mom claimed, "I'm too ignorant to worry!"

My dad had lived with fearful parents and was determined to break that cycle. He let us live our lives the way we saw best, offering opinions only when asked, and even then holding strong opinions in reserve.

"What do you think, Dad?" was countered by "What do *you* think?" Even Danny's death, which occurred on his watch, failed to undermine his determination to leave us in freedom. Instead, it confirmed his belief that the Lord calls us to the other world for much bigger reasons than we can see.

"Children are a heritage of the Lord,"[1] he told me more than once. He didn't own me, and he didn't want to restrict my ability to be free to make my own choices. Though he was passionate about our careers with delinquent teens, he always supported our sailing dreams and willingly transferred his eagerness for wilderness travel to the ocean setting. He helped us buy our boat and listened avidly to every detail. He thoroughly trusted Mark, and trusted our decisions.

Mark's feelings about departure were mixed. He was leaving a meaningful job and a work community that was close to family for him. He didn't want to stay there forever, but he still loved it. As a husband and father with a strong protective instinct, he deeply felt the responsibility of our wellbeing and financial survival. His parents and six siblings with all their families, busy with their own lives, quietly supported him though they were uninvolved with the details. Although Mark wondered if he was being irresponsible to be unavailable to his parents as they aged, they were used to his adventurous ways. His mom poured her love for us into a gorgeous nautical quilt for the girls. She brought it to us when they came to say good-bye.

We'd had some decent sleep by then. The girls raced up the dock and threw themselves into their grandmother's arms. She murmured softly.

"Yes, well. Are you ready to go?"

Cedar was bubbling with excitement. "Yes! Good-bye! Good-bye! It's happy and sad." She dragged Grandma in for a tour, and we laid the beautiful quilt down in the v-berth. The quilt would be a constant reminder of family love and support for our entire trip.

Grandma kept her tears to herself as she stood on the dock, holding Grandpa's hand. He waved jovially.

"Here you go!"

We pulled away from the dock.

"Good-bye! Good-bye!"

Even Lamar was calling it out. At twenty-one months she had no idea what was going on but sensed the excitement. Cedar was beside herself.

"We're not leaving the boat, and that is the truth!" She ran up and down the deck, waving. Lamar toddled behind. Soon the well-wishers faded into the distance. Cedar rushed to me.

"Mom, are we having cake for my birthday?"

There was a light breeze right on the nose. We put up the sails and slowly made our way forward.

* * *

Sailing departures can be short-lived. Weather, sea conditions, engine problems, and kid issues had forced us to turn back and try again more than once. This time, our departure held. Once we were off, we breathed the fresh air and felt our minds slow down. Cedar and I discussed her birthday cake. Should we dive into our precious store of chocolate chips? Mark sat in the cockpit, tiller in hand, his face a wreath of smiles. Lamar wandered the two-foot-square area behind him with her sippy-cup in hand. Everyone was happy, she could tell. She reached out and hugged Daddy from behind, and he swirled her around into his lap.

"What do you think, Lammie?"

She snuggled in, then wriggled off to explore again.

It took the girls about five minutes to adjust to life on a boat. For Mark and me, it felt easy and familiar. We were traveling through waters we knew like the back of our hands. It was days before we felt far from home. Our first few weeks were spent retracing our steps of the summer before, skirting the south shore of Lake Superior. The biggest difference was the size of the girls.

"It's so easy!" I remarked more than once. "They're both walking!"

There was one key difference, however. The pressure was off. Our only goal was to reach my family's vacation cottage on Lake Huron in a month or so to say our good-byes to them, then get to North Carolina by late fall. We had no return date, no mortgage or renters to look after, and virtually no bills. Our whole lives were now on the boat.

Note

[1]Psalm 127: 3.

Chapter Five

Overnights

Cedar was scratching again. Red welts, many of them bleeding, covered her little body. We were on Day Three of our trip and in the Apostle Islands on the southern shore of Lake Superior. We motored in a glassy calm to a rocky beach. It was hot—unusually hot for late June—and the water was crystal-clear. It was time for our favorite activity, one that soothed all types of red heat and restored energy—a cold-water dip.

We dinghied to shore and tentatively waded in. As expected, the water was frigid—probably around fifty-five degrees. Lamar retreated in shock. Cedar and I dunked together, holding hands. Whoosh!

"Let's do it again!" I gasped, thinking of the mosquito bites.

"One, two, three!" Cedar shouted and pulled me under.

Unable to resist, Lamar ran in and quickly dipped under. *Gasp!* She ran back out. Then in. Then out. Alive and tingling in every pore, I hustled out.

"It's like a combination of the best cup of coffee you ever drank, plus yoga, plus hearing really good news, all at once!" I tried to persuade Mark.

"I get goose bumps just watching," replied Mark, who kept a safe distance from the splashing. We watched the girls jump in and out. When they finally dried off for good, their lips were blue and they were shivering violently, cackling with laughter. The red welts on Cedar's body had shrunk and whitened. Maybe we'd get some sleep tonight.

Mark had brought the hand-held radio to shore and was listening to the forecast. He turned to me happily. "Moderate southwest winds all tonight and tomorrow!" he exclaimed as if he could hardly believe it. Lake Superior winds almost always change, or at least die at night. Our destination—Houghton, Michigan—was about a hundred miles away. Southwest winds would put us at a broad reach, our favorite tack. It would be our first overnight out on the water.

Mark and I had often fantasized about watching the sun go down on our tiny little boat, far from land. With the perfect forecast in front of us, children happy, parents rested, and all systems working as far as we could see, it was a good night to start. We pulled up the anchor as soon as the southwest wind kicked in, around suppertime. We were close to shore and the waves were mere ripples. I cooked macaroni and cheese, which we ate in the cockpit. Mark went down to do the dishes while the girls stayed up with me. There was plenty of light left in the evening.

"Time for bed!" I said enthusiastically. The girls looked at me expectantly.

"Are we going to sleep in the v-berth, Mommy?" Cedar asked. Instantly I knew that they could not. The v-berth was the bounciest berth.

"Um, no. You're going to sleep on the settees." Eyes widened in astonishment. This was going to be different!

Thus began the special rituals we would come to depend on each overnight as bedtime and darkness drew near. First, we set up sleeping bags on the settees with the lee cloths.

"Mom, don't forget this!" Cedar brought out her guardian angel, a piece of wrapped white cotton with a checked cloak. She'd made it herself. She hung it carefully over her pillow. We all rested easier knowing that angels were nearby. Then we read our standard two books, as the motion permitted, followed by prayers and songs. In the midst of the songs Cedar commented that she was "a tad seasick" and would like to come up for "a breath of air." Lamar was not to be left out; she was "a tad seasick, too." Twice they hopped out, glanced at the evening sun, and scurried back down the steps. Finally, they decided to stay put and I sat between them, singing, until all wriggling stopped. Ahh . . . I breathed easier. Now we just had to get through the night.

I had first watch. Mark was going to attempt an evening nap. As the sun sank slowly on this long, long late June day, it was so beautiful that I couldn't understand why we had waited so long to go out overnight. The forecast was so peaceful that we ignored traditional wisdom and left our light-air sail up, pulling us forward at three to four knots. It would be a bit complicated to bring down, but surely we wouldn't need to. The sun was setting bright pink, and the wind held. Waves of contentment washed over me as kindly as the murmurings of the water. This was what I had read about in all those sailing magazines! Could it really be this easy? I pulled out my headlamp to check the compass and learned my first lesson: our backpacking headlamps were too tiny for reading the compass or the telltales. The telltales, thin strings that hung from the rigging and fluttered in the breeze, told us our direction relative to the wind. Whenever I popped my head out of the hatch, the telltales were the first place I looked. They were simple, but utterly critical. Without them, I was totally disoriented.

Before I had time to consider what to do about my headlamp, the sail started flapping. We spun ninety degrees and began drifting downwind with a backed headsail. I called Mark, who had heard everything from below and was already getting his harness on. He jumped out, ran to the bow, and started pulling the cumbersome headsail down. The wind was blowing out of a completely new direction, and there was a small but rapidly growing set of clouds descending on us. It began to sprinkle. Um, what happened to light southwesterlies for the next twenty-four hours? While I fumed, Mark put up the regular jib and mizzen and we began to sail again.

"What's going on?" Cedar called from inside. "Daddy, why did you shut the front hatch? DADDY!"

"We're all good, Cedar—just a squall," I informed Cedar. Mark hung out with me for a while, then went back below. It was 11:05

p.m., and I was alone in the night. I was immediately confronted with everything I didn't know about sailing, or had forgotten. With light winds, we'd decided to try the autopilot, which began malfunctioning on cue when Mark went below. I tried to steer by hand, watching the compass with my dim headlamp. The wind kept changing directions, and it was easy to get disoriented. I saw red lights—a ship? Were they getting closer? I went down and checked the radar, pretty sure it was all clear—but maybe I wasn't using the radar correctly, either. Next, I saw a set of lights go across the front of the boat so quickly that I leapt into action, certain that something was moving right across our bow. Before acting on full-blown panic, I checked the compass. The lights weren't moving, but we were. There was nothing in front of us, but our wildly erratic forward motion had made it look as though there was. Ruefully, I steadied our course. The stars peeked out and rescued

Seasick.

me, helping me orient myself. I set the autopilot again, which seemed inclined to work this time.

I had hoped to go until 2:00 a.m. to give Mark a solid three hours of sleep, but at 1:00 the autopilot started ringing. I didn't want it to burn out, and I couldn't even figure out how to unplug it, so I woke Mark up. As he examined the autopilot, Lamar called, and I went below. After she went back to sleep, I took the helm one more time while Mark readied himself to be in the cockpit for the rest of the night. Then I went and lay down on the floor between the two girls.

In two minutes, Cedar needed to go potty. This accomplished, I lay down beside her, where I stayed in a slight doze for several hours. The gentle rolling was slowly building into something not so gentle. At dawn, Mark turned our bow through the wind, a maneuver known as "tacking." Heading straight into the waves bounced us heavily up and down. I knew I could get sick very quickly in these conditions and went out to eat crackers and touch base with Mark. We'd officially made it through our first overnight!

But we had no time to pin laurels on each other. Lamar woke up and I brought her outside in a blanket.

She nibbled a cookie but then threw it up. When Cedar woke, Mark bundled her up and got her outside. Lamar perked up the instant Cedar was in the vicinity, already chatty and triumphant. "We made it, Mom! Will you tell us a story?"

Slightly woozy, I tightened my grip on each girl beside me and dove in. "Did you know there is a Brownie living in *Amicus*? Well, one night he was hiding just behind the pots . . ."

Several elongated chapters on our personal family elf got us through the first few crucial hours. By mid-morning everyone was ready to move. Mark's oatmeal looked a lot better than it had earlier, and hot Ramen noodles followed the oatmeal. By lunchtime the girls were in the cabin turning somersaults on the settees, oblivious to the four-foot waves outside.

We blew into our river entrance, downed the sails, and turned on the motor for the first time in twenty hours. I went below and stared at the chaos. Did the girls leave any compartment closed? Sometime in the last hour Cedar had pulled out her art folder and opened its bag of glittering sequins. Either she just got careless, or a big wave had tossed the boat. The sequins were splayed all over the cabin, in every crack. She'd also started a knitting project, and the yarn ball had unrolled itself over books, crackers, paper, and glue. Crayons rolled up and down on the floor. *Stay calm*, I told myself. *They made it through a long day*.

Later, we negotiated. Cedar did not like the idea of cleaning up before anchoring, nor did she want her toy use curtailed. We compromised by designating a "passage toy bag," plus dolls, blankets, and pillows that could be used freely while underway. Other toys would be off limits.

We motored ten miles to Houghton, Michigan, and pulled into the dock just blocks from downtown. Mark and I found time for a quick high-five before responding to our seemingly tireless daughters, who were begging to head downtown.

"Mom! The library is *right here*!"

By late afternoon, exhaustion began to show.

"Time to go home," I told Cedar quietly in the library. She ignored me, lounging in an armchair, reading a book upside down. "I have to finish my chapter."

Eventually we got her out of there, kicking and screaming. An hour later, suppertime came. Cedar was rocking her dollies.

"They need to go to bed too, Mom."

At bedtime, it occurred to her that she could refuse the entire bedtime routine. She sat out on the settee in protest. Lamar lay wide awake in the v-berth, wondering what in the world would happen when Cedar was not there to go to sleep at bedtime. Mark and I looked at each other stupidly. Then we figured out that all we had to do was to lie down and turn out all the lights. There was a slight shuffle as (we hoped) Cedar found her way to the v-berth. Then, blessed silence. We had learned the basic truth about overnights: they are exhausting, but they are worth it.

After that we sailed overnight more regularly and enjoyed its advantages: sleeping kids, contemplative time alone, time to adjust to the motion, miles put away. Even though we were wiped out for at least one day afterwards, we gained many more miles than we would have by day-sailing only, and we could relax about entering new harbors and anchorages. Trying to get in before dark was stressful and had often forced us to motor when we could have sailed at a slower pace. Now, we could leave during the night and arrive almost anytime during the day. Sailing at night also fine-tuned our sensory awareness, and thence our sailing skills. We felt subtle wind shifts, smelled the teapot the instant the water was hot, and estimated wave height and boat speed by the sound against the hull.

If there was any "trick" to overnight sailing, it was to prepare well. Mark knew this. His hours of concentrated effort to secure every moving piece on the outside of *Amicus* calmed his spirit, raised his confidence, and assured him that he was doing his very best. Inside the cabin, I learned to be similarly vigilant. What might fall on its side? What might be dangerous and heavy? Did we need another bungee cord and hook? How full should the can locker be so the cans wouldn't shift too much? Was olive oil in a glass jar safe? Forethought eased our minds when conditions were worse, or different, than expected, or when regular wear and tear showed up on a passage. If we were jouncing along and heard an unfamiliar *clunk*, we all looked at each other and guessed. Oven door? Pressure cooker? Unlocked locker? It was fun, not worrisome. Preparation helped us feel that we were doing what we could—although we knew we could never cover everything.

* * *

Our next overnight was a couple of weeks later on Lake Huron. My family owned a cottage on the southeast shore, and we were going to sail down to it in one big overnight leap. Moreover, my dad was going to join us.

For some sailors, visits from family and friends were an integral part of their cruising journeys. For us, the size of our boat limited our options. With two side settees and one v-berth, we had few comforts to offer our guests, and no privacy. But we figured my dad could handle it.

He was the one who had taught me to rough it, after all. He was familiar with our boat, loved to sail, and wanted to be part of the action. My fervent hope was that Mother Nature would supply him with some wind.

My parents were scheduled to meet us in Tobermory, Ontario. For two days we sat on a government wharf, waiting and watching the weather for any sign of wind with an N in it.

There wasn't any, but that did little to dampen my spirits when I spotted my dad jogging briskly toward us in excitement, one hand holding his cowboy hat on his head. My mom followed behind with a calmer air.

"Katya!" Dad shouted, joy and pride bubbling out as he gave me a brief, tight hug.

I could hardly contain myself. "Dad—you made it!"

Were we really going to give my dad, the quintessential sailing enthusiast of my childhood, the longest sail of his life? Mark returned from the library where he'd just checked the forecast. He gave Dad a hearty handshake, then spoke soberly. "Well, do you want the good news or the bad news?"

Dad calmed down immediately. "Just tell it like it is."

The upshot was that we could leave first thing in the morning with barely manageable winds and a probable swell, or we could wait for something to improve, which didn't look likely. Thunderstorms were also heading our way. The decision was quick. We would leave at first light and bank on those potentially semi-favorable winds.

Mom left to drive down to the cottage, and my dad settled himself on board. By bedtime the girls had calmed down from the excitement and went to bed early, with special readings from Grandpa, who always brought new picture books. Dad lay down on the settee next to Mark and me. As the night wore on, I wondered if he was sleeping any better than we were. I doubted it. I knew his sleeping habits. I'd inherited them, in fact. There was too much noise, too much light, and too much excitement about what the day was going to bring. I felt transported back to the backpacking trips of my childhood.

Morning dawned with a thunderstorm and low-lying clouds. It passed and by 5:30 we were headed out into Lake Huron. Dad and

Mark were in the cockpit and I lay in the v-berth with the girls. Sleeping in was not an option, for those predicted swells got us up in a hurry. "Mommy . . ." Lamar moaned.

I grabbed her, swept up a blanket on the way out and bundled her up in the cockpit. Mark went back in for Cedar while Dad held the tiller. In minutes we were all watching the horizon. It was cloudy, but no rain forced us inside. When I brought out Cheerios an hour later, Lamar scarfed them down happily until her bowl was almost empty, then shouted, "I'm going to throw up!"

She expertly turned her head away from the cockpit and lost her breakfast, messing only the outer decks. As I threw a bucket of water over the decks to clean up, I marveled at the thought that seasickness need not be an emotionally miserable state. Was it possible to feel nauseous and not mind that much? Lamar was not about to be cheated out of her Cheerios and immediately dived back in.

We were heading south but the winds were distinctly southerly. There was a big swell coming up as well. All things considered, we were hanging in there. I had made a breakthrough in personal seasickness management. I had found my "special spot." I could occupy it for hours before having to move.

I leaned against the galley counter next to the companionway hatch. My eyes were on Mark in the cockpit. Both children, as long as they didn't venture into the v-berth, would be within a foot of Mark or myself. I had access to my box of crackers and any food Mark might want. I was beside the sink—handy for providing water and catching vomit. Most importantly, I could almost always see the horizon out the hatch. I could even cook quick meals, hang my head for a catnap, and make quick runs for the toilet, the fruit net, and the daughter lying on the settee. I could tell stories, discuss weather, and hear the radio. I stood in my special spot all morning. Cedar was busy organizing, I found out later as I routed out Ziploc bags of underwear, rocks, notebooks, doll clothes, and other random items stored carefully in odd places. It was a small price to pay for hours of quiet.

Picking blueberries.

By noon the conditions looked as though they were there to stay. *Amicus* was a beautiful boat, but she did not head close to the wind very well. We would have to widely tack, taking hours to make good every single mile. The other option was to turn on the motor. The swell was much stronger than the wind we were feeling, and our slow pace made the bobbing terrible. I was crushed. Dad was not getting his sail!

"Sorry, Dad." I gave him a rueful smile.

He chuckled. "Well—that's the way of it. You win some you lose some. I had a great sail with Mark this morning." Bowing to the inevitable, we turned on the motor, which brought unwelcome noise but a welcome relief from the bobbing around. I watched the girls, who were facing each other on the settee, all their passage toys lined up in front of them. "What are you up to?"

"Trade," replied Cedar, not looking up.

"Trade," echoed Lamar. I watched them. The purpose of the game was to trade, of course.

"How's it going?" I asked a minute later when nothing much seemed to be happening.

Cedar looked up. "Neither of us wants to give anything away!"

They were perfectly content, however, so I added a pile of peanuts each to the mix and returned outside.

That night, in a dead calm, we were still motoring. Cedar opted to stay up and watch the orange and pink sunset over the hazy horizon, cuddled next to Grandpa. We were accustomed to the noise of the engine by then and settled easily. Mark and Dad traded watches and the girls and I just slept. When we awoke at dawn, we were in a pea-soup fog and not far from the cottage. I was bristling with the same excitement I always felt approaching our beloved cottage with its familiar dark logs and low green hedge, tucked in behind the dunes. Only this time, I was approaching it from the water.

We slowed to a crawl and crept in toward shore. The fog thinned enough to reveal a hazy shoreline. Dad and I scanned with binoculars. "Is that it? Is that it?"

The girls caught the excitement. "Where's the family?"

My three sisters—Mary, Vera, and Lamar—and their families were all staying at the cottage. We hadn't seen any of them for a year.

"It's too early—they won't be looking yet!" I bemoaned.

The sandy shoreline sat peacefully empty except for a few seagulls and a lone figure walking a dog. Dad, looking through the binoculars, suddenly pointed.

"That's it! That's it!"

We all peered at the shore. The roof shingles were the right shade of green, the cottage comforting and familiar. Suddenly tiny ant-looking creatures seemed to emerge from the dunes and dance around.

Cedar asked, "Is that them on the shore?"

Black stick people waved toothpick arms with unmistakable gusto. Who else could it be? We waved back with equal fervor, then motored along to the harbor half a mile farther. They ran along the beach, dashed up the pier, and blew kisses at us as we rolled past.

The girls and I waved madly while Mark kept his eyes on the depth sounder and Dad perched at the bow, peering into the muddy water. This was the same pier I'd come careening into hundreds of times on *Sunlight*, including the time we lost the rudder so long ago. My memory was very clear that there were three solid feet of water in the channel. *Amicus*, however, was four feet deep. We were anxious not to follow in the footsteps of many infamous sailors (always big shots from Detroit "on a schedule," according to family lore) who ignored the yachtmaster's warnings to stay out of the channel until it was dredged, took off early on a Sunday morning, and promptly stuck fast in the sand. I remembered one boat owner who was so outraged to be trapped inside the harbor that he paced the decks of his boat and raged at anybody on the pier who would listen while a friendly tugboat captain tried (unsuccessfully) to free him. So I was grateful when we slid through the shallow section with only the barest nudge in the sand, which didn't even slow us down.

We pulled into our slip without mishap. Mark and Dad covered the sails while the girls watched for their cousins and I gazed across the channel at a rickety little dock right next to the big fishing boats, that had been home to our little *Sunlight* for decades. Although I'd loved *Sunlight*, living on a boat would never have occurred to me back then. Yet here we were, kids in tow, taking off for parts unknown from the very place where my intimate connection to the waves had been so deeply instilled.

My reverie was soon interrupted as "Hellooooo! There they are!" was shouted from across the channel, and the girls hopped onto the dock to receive honored guests and bask in the thrill of familial adoration and admiration.

Coming into Grand Bend.

Chapter Six

Family

We walked along the beach to the cottage in a daze. Breakfast was waiting for us—eggs, bacon, toast, and cold orange juice. The girls crowed with delight and fell to heartily while the cousins watched. Maya, two years older than Cedar, murmured, "What do they usually eat on the boat?"

And thus, our pace changed instantly. Suddenly we were on vacation! But wait—weren't we already on vacation? No, we realized, we were not. This was completely different. Our home was secure; other than allowing it to provide for our sleeping, we need not think about it. That alone changed everything for Mark, and he was able to relax for the first time in weeks. For me, having three motherly sisters nearby lightened my supervisory load to the point of giddiness. We could stop watching the girls' every move and let them disappear down in the dunes!

Which was what we did right after breakfast. My dad inspected every corner of the cottage. My mom did the dishes and peeked her head into the dining room, smiling contentedly to see her four daughters lingering, as always, at the breakfast table. Meanwhile, the husbands took care of the kids, picked the bathing suits off the ground and hung them on the hedge to dry, did the grocery shopping and the cottage repairs, and generally kept a low profile. They knew their duty, which was to empower their wives to spend as much time as possible in sisterly devotion to one another.

The days passed in a blur. It was boiling hot, and we slept in little sweat heaps on *Amicus* in the harbor, since there wasn't room for everyone at the cottage. The weather stayed hot and muggy all week, which kept us from our most cherished tradition, known in family lore simply as "Big Waves." When the crisp, cool, strong northwesterly winds brought in the brown, angry swells that broke over the sandbar, and the public beach was closed off with warning red ribbons, that was our cue to dive, goose bumps and all, straight into the madness and lose ourselves in the gritty, sandy breakers that repeatedly tossed us silly. My dad, of course, was the leader in these escapades. At his first Grand Bend visit five years before, Mark came down to the beach on the first day of Big Waves, took one aghast look, and hustled up to the cottage to fit the younger cousins with lifejackets. They would have none of it. I could appreciate Mark's comfort skiing up an ice-laden river, or climbing an exposed rock face, when we were playing in the great waves, happy as could be. Unfortunately, this was a year we did not get lucky.

One day Mark took advantage of the help from Steve, his handy brother-in-law, to paste sound-muffling panels around the engine, providing noise relief on *Amicus*. Cedar went along and brought Maya to the v-berth for some special time with their dolls. That night, Dad got out his guitar and sang the same songs to his grandkids that we sisters had heard a thousand times in front of the cottage's big stone fireplace.

"Sing 'The Fox went out on a chilly night' again, please, Grandpa!" they begged him. His eyes glistened and occasionally leaked over when the songs reminded him of Danny, whose picture in the smallest cottage bedroom showed him pulling the tiller of *Sunlight* over with that gleeful smile no one would ever forget. Cedar took Lamar into the room and pointed reverently.

"That's Uncle Danny, you know. He's in heaven, watching us."

Sunlight had been reluctantly sold a few years back, and we all missed waking up to the sound of Dad tapping the barometer over the fireplace and asking at breakfast, "Who would like to go for a sail today?"

So one evening, we took everyone out on *Amicus*. The winds were light and cool, and the grownups sat along the cabintop while the kids played inside. My sister Mary leaned back, letting the wind flow through her long, dark hair. "Ahhhh, this is amazing. I admire you so much—you are really doing it!"

Vera turned to me. "When, exactly, are you coming back?"

I scratched my head and looked at Mark. He was up at the bow, earnestly talking to someone else—probably answering the same question. "We don't know," I replied.

She nodded, but her eyes showed me that this was not enough for her. Behind the question was another unspoken one—was this all right with me? I gazed off at the horizon and wondered the same thing. At that moment, I wasn't sure what we were looking for. When would we know if we should turn back, or continue? What was going to determine our choices? Those questions would be answered on the journey.

I turned to my sister Lamar, who was seven months into her second pregnancy.

"We'll just see what happens," I said, patting her belly.

Was it possible that I would not see this little one for a year or more? Changes happened quickly with children.

Finally, the last morning was upon us. My family's enthusiasm and support of our trip made the departure all the more bittersweet. Mary, Vera, and I sat out on the lawn, trying to say our good-byes. We'd been through many emotional wringers together in recent years, not all of them comfortable. Mary hugged me, then looked me right in the eye as a silent tear rolled down her face. She had rarely played the role of caregiver, despite her status as the eldest, and this level of attention took me by surprise. My own tears started to flow. Vera, two years my senior, stroked my hand.

"Just know how much we love you and can't wait for your return," she said.

We all knew that no one had the time, money, or flexibility to take a family trip to visit us, wherever we were. Even if they had, we had no space to accommodate them. Except for a brief stop in Philadelphia to see Lamar one more time, this was it until we returned.

The departure itself was pure Goodenough—uninhibited and absurdly dramatic. Everyone ran along the pier, once again disregarding the cool demeanor of the average beach bather, and blew kisses our way as we motored out. Forced gaiety had replaced euphoric welcome, but tears were shed silently and brushed away as my family struggled to convey the fierce support and determined excitement that could come only from the deepest chords of love and loyalty. As we passed the end of the pier, various cousins leaned out over the water, still waving. My heart stuck in my throat. We waved and waved until our loved ones once again became tiny stick figures. Eventually they turned and walked away.

* * *

We turned our faces forward. The wind was not cooperating. Despite a favorable forecast, the waves were choppy and irregular and light winds came from all directions. Silently, Mark and I came to the conclusion that there was no point in putting up the sails. We would have to motor. I drew the girls beside me in the cockpit and held them close. After five days of land living, the girls and I were mildly seasick.

"I wonder what everyone's having for lunch?" Cedar commented. We speculated on each child's menu. "Crying, mom?" Lamar looked into my eyes. I brushed away a private tear.

"Just leaking, honey." Mark sat at the tiller and held down the fort, quietly as usual. I guessed that he was nursing somber thoughts of his own. Taking a woman far away from her sisters was a step no good husband took lightly.

About ten miles before we reached our destination, the wind picked up, blowing fresh air into the sails and into our sodden hearts. Suddenly, there was a new crisis. We had inadvertently raced a massive ore ship to the entrance of the Detroit River, realizing almost too late that we were closing in on the narrow entrance as quickly as it was.

"Quick—take the tiller," Mark said as he hurried down to check our bearing with the ore ship. A minute later, it motored into the river ahead of us, and we breathed easier. Mark took down the sails, and we started sliding downriver. The water turned muddy. In less than half a mile we had to turn into a tributary to dock for the night. The current swirled around us, and motorboats and jet skis were everywhere. This was a whole new ball game! My face must have illustrated my chagrin because the girls took one look and retreated below. Mark perched anxiously at the bow, directing me forward. We had no sooner made our turn into the tributary than a low bridge confronted us a hundred yards away. We would have to stop here, one way or another. Somehow I "parallel-parked" us at a cement wall between two three-story power cruisers, miraculously scraping no gleaming white fiberglass with our black steel. Mark leapt out with a rope and attached our bow and stern, avoiding any post-contact disasters.

"Whew!" I felt almost cheerful again.

After the excitement ended, my low spirits returned. It would be days before I could recover an optimistic heart and the spirit of adventure—particularly the brand of adventure that awaited us starting the very next day.

Chapter Seven

Engine Woes

The next morning was Saturday. We were parked right in the center of the action. Beach frenzy and motorboat traffic reached a crescendo by mid-morning as the population of northern Detroit decompressed from a mid-summer workweek. I tried not to stare back when bikinied beauties and bronzed warriors sauntered by and gazed at the cloth diapers hanging on the lifelines and our toddler-potty in the cockpit. We wanted to get out of there. But first Mark had to check the engine. He'd detected some warning mutters that prompted him to take a rag to the fuel injector pipes. Sure enough, they were leaking. He backed out of the engine compartment and told me, "We have a problem."

I wiped the sweat off my forehead and looked at him helplessly. "Could there be a worse time?" Just fifty miles away my sisters were starting to scramble eggs for a leisurely breakfast together, while we were stuck at a very expensive dock in muddy unswimmable waters on a Saturday morning, right when boat traffic was heaviest and mechanical support the lightest.

And here I must confess the nature of my relationship with our engine. Because we were not evolved to the level of Lin and Larry Pardey—world cruisers who lived on an engineless wooden sailboat— we'd succumbed to technology. In other words, our sailboat had an engine. I was alternately chagrined and tolerant of that brooding monster under the back hatch. It was like a dark habit that we couldn't break, but without which we doubted we could survive. It was old and not particularly responsive, which was most noticeable when we tried to go backwards. It was also loud and ugly and smelly—unlike Winnie our wind vane, a mechanical self-steering device that was silent, graceful, and efficient. Winnie went the extra mile with us when the winds were up. On the other hand, when winds were strong and we needed the engine to pull through, it groaned and slowed, sometimes holding us at a standstill. It had no ethics to dictate that it should not shut off without warning under the most dire conditions. I had experienced few challenges greater than maintaining basic human decency when the engine was malfunctioning.

It didn't help that my brain did not include any cells for understanding things like spark plugs and starters. Even looking at the engine from several feet away was enough to get my stomach churning. I fell prey to a sense of helplessness when challenged with a mechanical problem, and considered Mark's mechanical know-how nothing short of genius. However, my ears were perfectly attuned to detect the engine's slightest complaint. Occasionally I was the one who asked Mark, "What was that?"

Mark then tuned in and sensed instantly into which category the sound belonged: an emergency, not great but nothing to worry about until tonight, or irrelevant.

For instance, once when we were motoring along, my behind started to rattle. Mark obviously though silently concluded that there was nothing to worry about, even as it was rattling louder and louder. I thought my seat in the cockpit was going to vibrate my pants off, but I was too proud to ask about it when clearly Mark wasn't worried. In the evening, safely anchored and quiet, Mark casually entered the engine compartment and screwed the engine back onto the steel plate where the bolts had loosened. Not an engine problem at all—just a loose platform.

Another time, the engine sounded just a bit . . . insecure when he turned the key, but then started up just fine. I quickly put the engine-alert out of my mind and got ready to enjoy the day, while Mark glanced up in alarm and motored straight to a civilized dock before turning off the engine. Sure enough, we had a starter problem that led us on a journey of intermittent starts, manual cranking, and a final *kaput* a week later, which thankfully occurred near a park and a grocery store.

On that fateful morning in the Detroit River, the engine had been good for too long. I didn't trust it. After hearing the news I sat down and imagined the worst. It would be a long time before I was ready to start steering among million-dollar power cruisers in a current with a finicky engine.

Mark got on the phone, and soon had a mechanic on the line who promised to come Sunday morning. In the meantime, a guy who didn't look slick enough to be a weekend warrior approached the dock. "Hey, nice boat!" He began chatting with Mark. After a while we realized he wasn't going to wander away. Soon, we were discussing our life stories and, as an afterthought, the engine problem. Rob was a local with the week off, and he had friends in mechanical places. He drove us to get groceries. He promised to return in the morning to check our progress.

On Sunday, the mechanic came, put some sealant on the pipe threads, and said we were good to go. Traffic had diminished, and I felt potentially capable of maneuvering around three-story powerboats. Rob was there to see us off. "Thanks for everything!" Cedar called as he waved us away.

We motored a few miles, and then Mark checked the engine. It was leaking again. Without comment we pulled into another river, went under another bridge, and found another marina. Mark pulled out the cell phone. "Rob! Guess who?" This time Rob showed up with his diesel-mechanic friend. They eschewed the sealant as a waste of time and instead ordered pipes and spares, which would arrive in a few days.

So, once again we sat. "You know," Mark pointed out, "we ought to be grateful that this faulty pipe got us through eighty hours of motoring to land us in Detroit, home of the engine gods, before leaking." I grunted. Mark was spared my morose attitude when distress calls sounded below and I went to check it out. The girls were deeply immersed in troubles of their own. They had no name for the game they were playing, but I called it Negotiation. The purpose of Negotiation was to determine what game to play. It could last for hours as Lamar learned by trial and error how much sway she held as the younger sister, and Cedar developed ever-more complex means of orchestrating a solution that worked for both. "What are the options?" I asked them this time.

"I want to play Little House, but Lamar wants to play animals," Cedar cried unhappily. "She just won't listen to anything!"

Lamar looked at me and let out a string of indecipherable wailings.

Normally they would have worked this out. Surely Little House stories included animals—the pet dog, Jack, for instance. But when I made the suggestion, they both started in afresh. So I changed tactics. "We're going out," I announced.

"Where are we going, Mom?" asked Lamar from her seat in the jogger. "We'll just have to see," I answered and they sat back happily. After a few blocks of wandering, we were rewarded with a used-book store and a high school band camp. What could be better than seeing teenagers up close with tassels in their hair and golden instruments making magnificent noises? I even forgot for a while that sitting in the Detroit River was not the Plan.

Meanwhile, the engine wasn't through with us—not for several more days. We replaced the pipe. It continued to leak. Mark and the mechanic reassessed, ordered more parts, waited again, and installed more parts. By now, the entire fuel injector area was replaced and ready to go. But before leaving, Mark ran the engine for a while—just to see. Leaking! Apparently, replacing this pipe was a fine art. We waited for the mechanic to get back from lunch, and he came and tweaked it for another hour, assuring us we were truly good to go. More resigned than hopeful, we discussed our options. It was late; we were settled. We decided to wait for morning.

Besides, we had Rob to think of. He had driven across town to get the parts, discussed the engine problem with Mark from every possible angle, taken us out for ice cream and groceries, and put in some serious time listening to the girls. He was on vacation and had a seemingly bottomless supply of time and resources. So instead of leaving, we pulled out the barbecue and splurged on fresh avocado.

"Hey, you guys are really livin' the dream," he told us, not for the first time that week. "I really wish I could do that."

We sat under a pavilion at the marina and talked about our futures. "Rob," Mark said, "you should come sail Lake Erie with us."

Rob was all enthusiasm. "Hey, just give me a call!"

As it turned out, the engine truly was back in working order and we got all the way to Erie, Pennsylvania, without incident. Mark called Rob to invite him to visit. Exactly one week after we'd said good-bye, Mark dinghied over to shore to pick him up again. This time Rob was coming overnight. He ducked his head coming down into the cabin. He was too tall to stand up straight inside, so he sat right down. The girls eyed him shyly, already beginning to forget.

"How's your week been, Rob?" I asked as I drained the beans in the sink, filled the pressure cooker with water again, and sat it down on the stovetop.

"Oh, you know. Miss the kids and all."

Awkwardly I sat down across from him and the girls cuddled against me. I wondered about Rob's real life. Mark came down and gave him a hearty slap, breaking the silence. "Rob! You're livin' the dream!"

When we went to bed that evening, we were reminded how intimate were our quarters. Rob was a snorer. It was a loud night. Still, the next day, after a good sail, Mark invited him to come sail for longer down the East Coast.

Rob's eyes clouded. "Yeah, I will. I will. Just give me a call."

When we waved good-bye the next morning, he waved back from the dinghy. But this time his face was sad and his wave wistful. We lost touch after that. Mark had set him up with email, but, as he explained, Rob wasn't the "emailing type."

Chapter Eight

Eastward

A few days later we were sailing hard and fast on the eastern side of Lake Erie. Notorious for its choppy waves and shallow waters, Lake Erie ended abruptly with a breakwall right in downtown Buffalo, New York. Twenty-five-knot winds behind us had made for glorious sailing in steep, eight-foot waves.

Lake Erie.

The city was visible from miles away, but there was no channel to enter. From a distance it appeared that we were going to crash right into the breakwall and its city sidewalks, but Mark assured me after studying the charts that a series of barriers and buoys gradually broke up the waves. I tried to trust that things would settle down by the time we got closer. Mark peered through the binoculars. Every few minutes he directed me. "I see a red light to the right! Head left—"

It had been a long day. Cedar was harnessed into the cockpit. Storytime had been rudely cut short when both Mark and I were needed to steer and navigate. Usually the girls could sense when it was a terrible time to make a scene, but every now and then their fuses ran short at the worst moment.

"What's the name of the cow, Mom?" Cedar hollered repeatedly in my ear, successfully penetrating my concentration. She was referring to the cow whose life story I had stopped reading minutes before.

I shouted, "Hendrika!"

Cedar settled down again with her book but Lamar poked her head out of the hatch. "I have to be with Mommy!"

She started teetering toward me. In about three seconds, Mark put on her harness and tossed her to my lap, where I held her in an iron grip with one hand, the other on the tiller.

"We're getting close," Mark said. "I'm going to start taking down the sails." With a harness attaching him to the jacklines along the deck, Mark carefully staggered out to the mast and pulled down the main sail. Instantly we slowed down and tossed more in the waves. He wrapped his arms around the boom to hold himself in place as he tied the sail down.

Cedar started to teeter over to her dad but I cut her short. "Stay over here, honey." I held tightly to the girls' harnesses to keep them away from Mark who strained and grunted at the winches.

Sailing in on the jib alone, it was time for the moment of truth, a moment that neither Mark nor I ever discussed but which we both felt keenly. Mark went below, stuck the key in the engine starter, and turned. Without hesitation the engine started. I felt instant gratitude. Even with fuel and oil and water all bouncing around in there, the engine had pulled through for us! I gave Mark a goofy smile.

"Buffalo, here we come!" I cried.

The girls giggled. "Daddy?" asked Cedar thoughtfully. "Do you think you can make me a laptop computer?"

Mark was watching the horizon. The big puffy clouds along the shoreline were fast developing. Suddenly they looked dark and stormy. We rolled sideways off a big wave, nearly flooding the portholes as a crack of lightning and its attendant thunder boomed over the city. With all barriers behind us, the breakwall loomed ahead. The waves were down, but I wouldn't have called it calm by any stretch.

"I have it!" Cedar decided. "I'm going to make myself some pumps! Mom, can I pull out the blocks?"

She headed inside, Lamar following her down. Soon Cedar poked her head up. "Lamar wants to make a trombone, but she needs Daddy's help."

"Just tell me when," I said to Mark as firmly as I could manage. As we came up to the break wall, he pulled hard on the jib, winching it in grunt by grunt. As the last foot of sail disappeared into the roller furling, he hollered, "Okay!" and I turned a fast corner. One, two waves hit us from the side, but then we were behind the breakwall, protected from the full brunt of the Lake.

"Whew!" I managed by way of congratulations, but it wasn't over yet. We were still bouncing heavily and moving too fast for comfort. So far we had not used the engine, and it sat idling.

Mark contacted the marina by radio and directed me to a dock where a couple of young guys were waiting for us. The current and waves were bouncing us right by. We came in roughly and threw them our lines, which they held in their hands, ignoring the cleats. A surge was rolling us around, drifting us away from the dock.

"Put it around a cleat!" I yelled.

"Nope," one guy answered. "I broke a rope that way earlier today." I groaned inwardly. Finally they got us close enough to shore that Mark hopped out and took charge.

"Hey, we need to get out of the surge. Where can you put us?"

The boys responded well to his captain-like authority and willingly checked their marina diagram again. Soon we were headed for a narrow slip way down at the end of the dock. I could not envision how we would fit, but Mark was calm as ever.

I tried not to shout frantically at onlookers who stood watching this circus act. I kept it short and positive. "Fend us off!"

It took about four friendly adults on the docks to keep the boat from hitting anything, but we slid into our spot with over a foot to spare on either side.

"How was the sailing?" one of the onlookers asked Cedar, who had emerged again to watch the fun.

"Great!" she responded.

Mark and I focused on attaching ourselves to the dock. We were parked right on a scenic sidewalk. Decompressing was going to be a public event. The girls wriggled out of their harnesses and ran inside for their anchoring treats. Mark put the sailcovers on the sails and tidied up all the lines. I replaced cushions, books, and blankets below, then examined food lockers to see if anything had spilled or broken.

In a few minutes, I put a pot of water on to boil and pulled out cans of tuna. Tuna Wiggle, as we called that comfortable noodle casserole, seemed a fitting celebratory meal for tonight.

Mark came down. "Tuna Wiggle?" His voice was glad. He drank a quart of water and then helped Cedar duct-tape blocks to the heel of her shoe.

"Mom! Look at the pumps I made!" She traipsed about on the sidewalk.

Then Mark and Lamar found two sticks that could be wound together with a rubber band. When she slid them up and down and blew into the ends, it did suggest a trombone. Pedestrians walking their dogs cheered as Lamar marched up and down with her new instrument. One woman who had watched our dramatic arrival leaned over and waved frantically at me inside.

As she turned away, I heard her murmur, "She's cooking! Amazing!"

I laughed inwardly, the tension released inside. *If she only knew!* I thought. We had successfully crossed the Great Lakes. That was the amazing part to me.

Chapter Nine

New York

W hen I had nightmares about cruising, it was never about big waves or storms. Instead, we'd be trying to steer *Amicus* down a main street in a fast river with dwindling water. I could see the dry land ahead, and I charged forward into certain disaster, hoping against hope that our momentum would carry us through. Such dreams, I know, come from those times of motoring in narrow channels, far from big water.

Between lakes, we'd slid down both the St. Mary's and Detroit rivers. After Buffalo, we entered the Erie Canal, a waterway originally dug for westbound settlers that took us through the heartland of New York. On the Erie Canal, we could bypass the much longer route up the St. Lawrence Seaway and come into New York City in two weeks, or even less.

We were sold on the idea, so a few days after we blew into Buffalo, we took off for the nearest boatyard. The canal went under hundreds of low bridges; our masts would have to come off. A do-it-yourself crane hung right over our dock. I set up the girls with a painting project at a nearby picnic table, then cranked the crane up and down while Mark attached the first mast to it. We swung it carefully into a horizontal position and laid it as gently as we could on homemade crutches. The girls left their painting after about two minutes for the more unique pleasure of watching their parents dodge swinging masts, roll halyards, and pad up and tie down our precious masts. Soon, the masts were immobilized like broken legs across our cabin top, pointing dangerously out in front of the bowsprit.

We woke, we checked the forcast, we motored.

Without masts, we were denied many of our modern and ancient comforts. The antenae at the top enabled the SSB radio and our radar. Other useful tools hung from the mast, like the compass, our solar shower, and our shade-providing awning. We became completely dependent on the engine again. After a couple of hours of travel we found ourselves in a narrow, weedy channel, miles from any sizable body of water. Slowly we adjusted from our lives as windblown voyagers to tourists aboard our own personal ferry. I had to admit, there was a charm about this new life—a calmness that came from being able to predict, approximately, what was going to happen every day. We woke; we checked the forecast; we motored.

Without navigational tools, we trusted that the canal was going where it told us it was going. The most exciting pastime was observing the backyards of rural Americans. We watched countless New Yorkers in the privacy of their own yards doing everything from hanging up laundry to getting married. We were recipients of many friendly waves and occasionally got up close and personal with folks who had nothing to do with the nautical life. It was refreshing.

The journey was broken up frequently with one of the thirty-five locks that brought boats from the Midwest over 500 feet down to sea level. We had traveled through a very large lock for ore ships a few weeks ago when exiting Lake Superior. Nothing terrible had happened, but the sheer amount of water swirling out of the lock as we dropped was intimidating. *Amicus* seemed tiny and vulnerable next to the massive ships. So we felt wary as we put-putted our way into the first lock on the Erie Canal. A green streetlight at the gate told us when the gates were open. Once inside the lock we gently nudged up to the wall. Since we were going down, we started high, looking out over the land. The lockmaster directed us to our spot and threw us yellow ropes to hold on to to keep us in place. I held the rope while Mark stood at the tiller. I also held the boathook to fend us off the wall if we started moving. In a minute we slowly started to drop. Water swirled gently around us, entering the lock from some unseen source. Mark's face cleared, and I let out a breath of relief. This was going to be easy. It was designed for small boats like ours

Coming through the locks.

rather than ore ships. No swirling current would twist and turn our boat, or shove it roughly against the wall.

The girls watched, fascinated, as the walls around us grew higher and higher. "Where are we going?" Cedar asked.

"Down," said Mark.

In ten minutes the walls around us were fifteen feet high and we were alone in the world. The gates at the far end slowly opened and we knew we were through. "That was fun," said Cedar as she dived below. On the way out I waved and smiled at the lockmaster.

One late afternoon as we passed through a lock, we pointed to the staging wall and asked, "Can we stay here for the night?"

"Sure, sure," the lockmaster answered with a friendly smile. As soon as we were settled we saw him waving to us from the lock, and we wandered over to chat. The girls were fascinated with his long black hair and traditional Native dress.

"Do you want to see how the lock works?" he asked them. Mutely, they nodded and reached for our hands. He showed us the huge red cranks and wheels. All he had to do to bring the water up was turn the shiny red crank. This would open an underwater culvert from the "high" side, letting water into the lock, which was a fixed chamber. When the water level reached that of the "high" side, he then cranked open the upper gate. To lower a boat, the process was simply reversed. The girls absorbed the miracles of mechanical advantage as they watched. It was all obvious to Mark, but amazing and beautiful to me. How could he move so much water so easily? We had lost something in the age of computers, of that I was sure.

An early summer storm had damaged many of the locks. This one had just been repaired a few weeks before. Slabs of cracked concrete lay in a huge pile of rubble nearby. I asked the lockmaster about his job. We had never had to wait for a lockmaster. Did he ever get a break? He looked at us and smiled.

"There's three of us for each lock. The boss, who works business hours, and then two Indians"—he winked—"we work the rest of the time."

* * *

New York! The city loomed ahead of us, skyscrapers as far as the eye could see on both sides of the Hudson River. The engine was on, the tide was with us, and we were coming down into it at eight knots. It was early September, eighty degrees, and humid. The air was hazy and thick. Mark had just installed a cockpit table, and the girls were water-color painting outside, clad only in their underwear.

"Look up!" I told them. "Paint the skyline!"

They looked up for a few seconds, then looked down again, absorbed in painting apples and trees.

Soon a series of bridges loomed ahead. We were arriving. We crumpled up the paintings, and I tossed a bucket of water over the table to clean it. Water flowed down and out, and Mark quickly unscrewed the table. Easy on, easy off.

I stepped below to find the girls a snack. We would be occupied for a while, so I pulled out two precious juice boxes and handed them up, along with leftovers from breakfast: two bowls of cold oatmeal with raisins.

The girls gasped with delight at the juice boxes. "Thanks, Mom!"

They planted themselves on the cabintop—the life raft their backrest, the folded dinghy their seat. Cedar took a bite of oats, and then a sip of juice. Lamar watched carefully, then followed suit.

Mark had done his homework and knew where in this mass of noise, exhaust, and humanity we were headed. We bounced under a bridge clogged with eight-lane traffic and beside powerboats of all shapes and sizes, plus a few luxury liners with helicopter pads on top. Helicopters flew overhead at regular intervals. The current and tide moved us swiftly forward.

"Over here!" Mark shouted from the bow.

I turned to the side and ferried us at an angle into what looked like a bunch of sailboats bobbing in the current. As we closed in, small mooring balls became visible. I tried to nudge up to one, but I was coming at it from the wrong angle, and we went sliding past. Mark came back and took the tiller, swinging us around. We headed upstream toward a mooring ball on the outskirts of the mooring field, and there I successfully hooked a ball. I passed our rope through its metal loop and cleated it at our bow. Then I straightened up and looked around. We were in the land of the Big Apple.

The next morning we went to find out what New York was all about. First, we had to get to shore. Our safe, out-of-the-way mooring, as it turned out, was very far from the dock. The current, the switching tides, and boat traffic all had their say in the water's motion around us. Mark firmly tied the dinghy to the side of the boat. Lamar, ready in her lifejacket, was so eager to get in she leaned over the lifelines, got the waistline of her lifejacket caught on the rail, and did a somersault into the dinghy. By the time I moved to catch her it was too late. She looked up at me and smiled. Cedar, as always, had a comment. "Whoa! What was that?" She climbed down after her.

Mark picked up the oars before I came down.

"My turn," I reminded him. I loved the chance to get a little exercise. Twenty minutes later, I was still hauling and pulling.

"Okay, I'll switch," I grunted.

Mark jumped up and took my spot. It took him ten more minutes to complete the 300-foot journey to the dinghy dock against the tide. We watched other boaters, moored much closer and with outboard motors on their dinghies. "Next time we'll watch for a favorable tide," I assured Mark.

He grunted in response, "Maybe we do need an outboard."

Once we made it to the dinghy dock, we had only to go through the black iron security gate, dodge bikers, walkers, and runners, and cross one busy highway. Then we found ourselves in downtown Manhattan, just a few blocks from the subway and Central Park.

We decided to head to Ground Zero, but getting there on the subway was an experience in itself. A train underground! Homemade map on one knee, Cedar loudly explained to her dolly where we were, to the amusement of a few people who raised their eyelids. The subway jerked. Cedar fell over onto a man dressed in rags, a little drool rolling down his stubbled chin. He looked down on her and smiled. Cedar beamed. "Good thing someone was there to catch me!"

We successfully exited the subway, climbed up to the street, and were immediately stumped. Mark and I studied the map, a girl securely fastened to each hand. A bus stopped by us and we studied it. Could it be the right one? We hopped on. A dark-haired woman in a black business suit behind us took pity on us. "Where are you headed?"

When we told her, she laughed and pointed. "It's right there— just walk!" We hopped back off the bus. Before we completed our journey, a young woman with pink hair and a leopard shawl approached us. "You look like you need help. Where are you headed?"

Finally, we made it to Ground Zero. Layers of barbed wire fencing separated us from the site, which was simply a few blocks of construction deep underground. The girls were interested in the vendors selling paraphenalia, but Mark and I took a few moments to reflect on the site where disaster had struck five years before. A few buildings nearby had blackened sides, the only visible scars of the fateful terrorist attack. Somehow, we'd arrived there on September 10.

Next, Times Square. Again we sat anxiously at a bus stop until a large dark man with long beaded dreadlocks and bright striped flowing skirts saw us studying our maps. "Can I help you find your way?"

With his assistance, we were deposited by bus at the corner of Times Square. New Yorkers strode by us in business suits, or sashayed by chatting in dungarees, or stood playing music or selling food or handing out pamphlets. Was it possible for just one human race to have such wildly varying skin, hair, clothes, expressions, strides, and mannerisms? The girls just stared. We put them on our shoulders and walked a block or so, passing the massive blinking billboards that we decided made up Times Square.

"Enough?" I looked at Mark. He nodded. We hopped on the next bus going out. We could do without the billboards, and we could see people anywhere in the city.

Mark had a wad of cash in his pocket. It was our designated "fun money." All the cash gifts we'd received for years had gone into it. Finally we were ready to spend it. Museums and entertainment awaited. But first, refrigerated and prepared food. The girls slurped coconut and pineapple ices, the most delicious street food any of us had ever eaten. We ate lunch at an Indian restaurant and rested our legs.

In the afternoon we made our way to a playground in Central Park, which was crowded with hundreds of children. Mark and I collapsed onto a park bench. "Go play!" we told the girls.

Lamar sank into my lap and fell asleep. Cedar watched the action. "Will you play with me?" she asked Mark.

"In a few minutes," he murmured, his head nodding sideways. As soon as Lamar awoke, we put the girls back on our shoulders and headed out. It was getting late, and we walked slowly. I remembered the swirling current and the long, hard dinghy ride that lay ahead of us. We had a bag of freshly bought fruit and vegetables in our backpack, but we were weak with exhaustion. We looked up. Glittering golden arches blinked above us, and that familiar smell of deep-fried grease that rises in every town in the United States wafted our way. Our boycott of fast food and everything it stood for disintegrated. Mark muttered, "Shall we?"

With a quick nod, we ducked in and bought enough cheap, processed protein to get us back home.

Back at the dock, we searched for our dinghy among the dozens tied there. Mark untangled our line from all the others and brought the dinghy over. We got the girls into their lifejackets, and they hopped aboard.

We gazed out at the river. The tide had switched since we rowed in that morning. We would be rowing against it again. And this time we had the natural current pushing us backward as well. Mark looked at me. "I think we should study the tidal charts next time."

He jumped in, grabbed the oars and heaved mightily toward the shoreline, where the current was weakest. Inch by inch he pulled us upriver while the girls and I watched, unable to lend a hand. Bikes and joggers passed us on the sidewalk just above our heads. The time it took to switch rowers would have lost us more ground than we stood to gain, so I didn't offer to trade places.

We came parallel to *Amicus,* but she was way out in the current. Mark kept rowing. When he was satisfied that we would not get swept past *Amicus* before we could reach her, he turned slightly and headed into the swirling waters. He pulled swiftly upstream and out, and the current grabbed us. We were sliding downstream but not too fast. All Mark's years of canoeing in moving water served him well. He had judged it exactly right. We reached *Amicus*'s hull and I grabbed the lifelines. Mark let go of the oar and grabbed too, just before we swirled out and downriver.

"Get out!" I tried to be pleasant. Cedar jumped up and stepped onto the ladder. Lamar teetered across my lap, a hand on my shoulder, then stepped up. I helped her find her footing.

Back on board, it was getting dark. As dark as it gets in New York City, anyway. Helicopters flew overhead every few minutes.

Reaching the Atlantic.

Surely there weren't that many emergencies, even in New York! "Why all the helicopters?" I wondered aloud.

"It's all the CEOs going to and from meetings," Mark guessed.

Of course! I looked back at Manhattan. "Look, girls!" A bright light was shining straight out of the ground and swooping through the sky.

Again, Mark had the answer. "It's right at Ground Zero. I bet it's commemorating 9/11."

We watched the action for a few minutes and headed below. It was too bouncy to do much, and we'd lost our sea legs. Exhausted and headachy, we headed straight to bed.

Turns out, it was as hard to leave New York City as it was easy to arrive. It was the height of the hurricane season, something we'd never had to worry about in the Midwest. Low front after front marched across us, each threatening storm or hurricane status. After a few days of city life, we were ready for a slower pace. We eventually made our way a few miles downriver to Sandy Hook, a cruiser's enclave in New Jersey. There we met new sailing families, rested, and prepared to meet the Atlantic Ocean.

Mama sailing the Atlantic.

Chapter Ten

The Learning Curve

Some weeks later, we were anchored at Cape May, the southern tip of New Jersey. We were feeling good. We'd just sailed 100 miles down the Jersey shore—our first experience on the Atlantic Ocean. We now knew a bit about ocean swells, which made all the difference in our confidence. There are two types of movement in the ocean. Local, current winds created waves similar to those of the Great Lakes, except that they were generally farther apart and easier to handle. Underneath these waves was the ubiquitous ocean swell—often imperceptible unless you focused on the horizon. These swells came from thousands of miles away.

We were not lulled by their gentle undulations. We knew they were sleeping giants, harmless until they woke up. Given enough wind, these swells could become real, live monsters. The sheer amount of water behind each swell sent shivers up my spine. Just imagining what a swell one-fourth mile wide and thousands of miles long could do if it became a wave was enough to inspire caution—caution that kept us close to shore and even dictated that we sit for several days at Atlantic City, spending $128 per night on a marina that offered us no actual people—just showers, hundreds of empty powerboats, and access to a massive casino and mall.

After three days in Atlantic City, the forecast had turned favorable, and we sailed the rest of the way to Cape May. Here we awaited southeasterly winds that would enable us to head northwest up the Delaware Bay—an area famous for its strong tidal current. We had been repeatedly warned by other sailors: "Don't even think about going out there if there's any 'w' in the forecast." The danger was in experiencing winds that ran against the tide, inevitably creating a terrific chop. Well . . . the forecast was for light winds, with perhaps a touch of west in them. We were back in coastal waters. How bad could it be? The other consideration was the tide, and it was in our favor. It would carry us up into the bay for most of the day.

There were several other boats anchored near us. We motored out bright and early. I noted our fellow sailors' lack of ambition.

"Look," I cried, "we're the only ones taking advantage of the day!"

They were all sleeping in and would miss this excellent opportunity. By the time breakfast was finished, we were out in the bay. A light northwest/west wind sprang up, and within minutes steep waves crashed into our bow. My gloating face was wiped clean.

I sat in the cockpit, a girl on each arm, watching Mark, who was watching the horizon. Half an hour later a couple of waves put the bow completely under water, and we stopped moving forward. Cedar lost her breakfast over the side. Without a word Mark turned around.

We were always wary of "the herd mentality"—doing something only because everyone else seemed to be doing it. But we had to admit, sometimes there were good reasons why people were doing what they were doing. We were new kids on the block, and it showed. The next day, we tried it again with about twenty other boats. We rode the tide on glassy seas all day and arrived in the Chesapeake Bay.

The next day, the pace changed again. My sister Lamar in Philadelphia was a mere two-hour drive away. She was due to have a baby any minute. She had faithfully attended both my births in northern Minnesota, and I was holding onto a secret hope that a well-timed visit would coincide with the family's newest arrival. We left *Amicus* in a marina and an old friend came and picked us up. But after three days in Philadelphia, we started to get anxious. The birth did not appear to be imminent. The daily marina fee was starting to add up. We discussed different plans, none of which proved practical.

Lamar finally smiled at us wanly. "I think you should go. It'll be all right." So we left. I gave Lamar a silent hug and felt like a shmuck. She looked ready to cry.

A day later we were on the cell phone, and things were happening. Lamar's contractions were real now. We were in the north end of the Chesapeake Bay, with few roads in sight. I was frantic. I made plans and discarded them. We owned a chart, but no map. It was doubtful that any buses came down this way. Even if we could dock at a town and find a ride, it would take four hours to drive back to Philadelphia—too long in the birthing world. I cried silently in the cockpit. Cedar came out. "Why are you crying, Mom?"

I brushed the tears away. "Oh, my sister is having a baby and I'm not there, is all." We anchored and lost cell phone coverage. I silently put bread and peanut butter, carrots, and apples on the table. We ate quietly.

We spent the next day on the shore, despite a perfect sailing wind. Mark played with the girls on the beach while I combed the nearby fields of hay, searching for cell phone coverage. Finally I got through. The phone rang at my sister's house and my mom picked it up.

"Yes, Lamar has a baby boy!" But her voice held a twinge of hesitancy. Something was not right.

"How are they?" I asked breathlessly.

"Well . . . fine. Fine. But Lamar had some problems, and they had to move her to another hospital."

"What!? How bad are the problems? Who's with Lamar? When will she be back with her baby?" Shaking, my fingers wrote the phone number for the hospital.

I called, and miraculously got Lamar right away. She sounded groggy and exhausted. "I'm not sure where I am," she murmured. "Or where the baby is."

I clenched my fingers. Could my sister have needed me more? She was alone in a hospital without her baby! After talking to her, I sat down in the field and cried my heart out.

I found out later it wasn't as bad as it sounded. Barrett, her husband, was with the baby, and the midwife did not rest until baby and mama were reunited, which took a few hours. The issues that had necessitated a move to a surgeon healed in good time. "In the end, I just wanted to labor alone anyway," she told me. "It was fine, really."

But I couldn't believe her, and I didn't forget for a long time that I had missed the once-in-a-lifetime opportunity to be present at my nephew's birth and provide invaluable support to my only little sister. Could I pay attention to anything else while we sailed, or was the life of a liveaboard simply too absorbing? With great caution, Mark patted me on the back. "You never would have made it to the birth had we lived in Minnesota, either."

I looked at him. He was right. We sisters had settled across the country from each other; even when we lived on land, visits had been annual at best. Lamar had managed open-ended visits to my births because she didn't yet have children. Maybe this was forgivable after all. I tried Mark's line and even shrugged my shoulders like him. "What can you do?"

It helped—a little. We moved on.

* * *

From the Chesapeake Bay we headed south. The Intracoastal Waterway, or ICW, flows inland all the way from Virginia to Florida—safe, but unexciting. One lovely evening as we motored along, a brilliant orange sun slipped down directly in front of us. With civilization so close by, we'd gotten complacent and were without an official plan for the night. We hoped simply to pull out of the channel and anchor when it got shallow. Unfortunately we didn't even try until sunset.

Within ten feet of leaving the channel we ran aground. This would never do. We needed at least a little swinging room, and anchoring in the center of the channel would be foolish. We reversed hard and the muddy water swirled around us. Soon we were free. We continued onward, anxiously scanning the sides of the channel for a possible place to rest while the dark descended. The girls were below, and from the sounds of it, things were going downhill fast. I heard a crash and a scream—an angry scream, not an in-pain scream. "MOMMMM!!!!"

The rising tension, the howls, the gorgeous sky—it all felt so familiar. How? Suddenly I felt transported back fifteen years. I was leading a backpacking trip in the mountains, and we couldn't find a place to camp. The adolescent girls trailing behind me were in various phases of meltdown.

"Just like the old days!" I called up to Mark, who understood instantly. Like then, we ignored the rumble and stayed focused on the task at hand.

Just as it was getting too dark to see, we passed a piling off to the left, and an old wharf. Mark instructed me to turn around and nose into the piling at such an angle that the stern would swing toward the wharf.

I gingerly turned out of the channel and nudged us into the piling, and Mark threw a rope around it. He instantly estimated how much line to let out at the bow, then dashed back to the stern with another line, climbed lightly on the solar panel frame, and instructed me to slowly reverse. When I was within a foot of the wharf, he jumped off, ran the line through something, and threw the other end to me. He then jumped aboard.

It was too dark to see by now, but we were out of the channel, securely tied, and not aground. We were essentially parallel-parked between the channel and a backyard. We could see bright lights and a TV blaring in the living room adjacent to the backyard. No one came out to ask what the heck we were doing there.

"It's a good thing you're so good at getting us out of pickles!" I remarked. I was giddy with relief as I descended into the cabin.

A makeshift concert greeted me below. Lamar was deep in reverie, her cardboard fiddle dancing at her chin. Her wrist loosely drew the bow across the strings in perfect imitation and her voice lustily let loose. Cedar sat nearby with her cardboard guitar. A book of *Peter Rabbit*, serving as sheet music, was propped up in front of her. She delicately turned the page with her foot as she strummed, keeping her eyes glued to the music. Whatever had been the problem a few minutes ago, they had recovered. I smiled and listened to the concert.

"Anyone want to see the stars?" Mark's voice came from outside. They jumped up, ran out, took a passing glance at a brilliant night sky, and returned to the cabin. It was almost frosty out. Time for a quick but filling dinner—fried potatoes browned with lentils and ground beef, carrots, and celery. A fried egg on top completed the meal. We ate lustily. Unbearable heat in Canada, and now a deep chill in Virginia. What would we find next?

Chapter Eleven

Marriage as Captain and Crew

A few mornings later, the cabin slowly turned gray as light reluctantly found its way through the portholes. Mark got up and quietly turned on the forecast. I lay in the v-berth with the girls and listened to the crackle of the radio over their deep breathing. We wanted—badly—to get out on the ocean and sail overnight as we headed south along the coastline. We needed to get out there with a favorable tide, and return in with a favorable tide, and also during daylight hours. Inlets were few and far between. We could not let our speed drop below five knots without risking an entrance into an unfamiliar inlet after dark. More than twenty knots of wind could build the waves considerably, but not enough wind was bad too. Motorsailing on a port tack risked overheating the engine. We had taken our Dramamine, but the girls had been up at night and no one had slept well.

Mark came and leaned on his elbows at the base of the v-berth. We sat quietly, listening to the girls breathe. He rubbed my toes through the blanket, then spoke. "Well. That's new. He wasn't saying anything about twenty-five knots before."

The eternal optimist, I had my answer ready. "Yeah, although it's fifteen to twenty-five—probably just gusty."

Mark considered. "Hmmm, except thunderstorms are in the picture now."

"Yeah, but the wind direction is more easterly now, which is a slightly better angle."

"Not much better. It wouldn't take much to be on the nose."

Indirect conversations like this drove me crazy. "You don't want to go out, do you?"

Mark's voice took on an edge of frustration. "Well, what do *you* want?" At this moment Lamar's eyes opened wide. We smiled at her, trying to lay aside our frustrations, but unable to release the tension between us. It was time to start the day, but what kind of day would it be?

Sometimes people wondered aloud what was most difficult for Mark and me on a sailboat. Usually they never guessed. Tiny living space? No problem. We were used to tents. No hot water? Just use the kettle and forget about the rinse. Poop spilling into the pee bucket? Put on gloves, plug your nose, and the deed is done. Broken parts or mysterious malfunctions? Just take it apart and have a look.

But when and where to go each day—now that was hard. Hidden in the question of whether to take off or not were hundreds of unspoken others: how much did we trust each other's judgment? How did we feel about pain, and fear? What level of stress felt unbearable? How badly did we want to leave? What would everybody think about our decisions? And what would we do when we disagreed?

This issue had existed between us ever since we began sailing together, an intricate web of love, fear, confidence, and trust that surfaced in frustrating and debilitating ways. As we zeroed in on our first huge goal—reaching Beaufort, North Carolina, in time to set ourselves up for an offshore passage to the eastern Caribbean—the tension was mounting. I leaned on Mark for vision, and his vision had always been to go offshore voyaging. I knew how competent he was and had an almost childlike faith in his ability to weather whatever came our way. But Mark was talking to a lot of people, and coming to the conclusion that this passage to the Virgin Islands was not an easy one, and not necessarily a prudent choice for a first-time family.

A few weeks before, he'd approached me with a new idea: how about his doing it with a couple of crew, and the girls and I flying out to meet them once they got there? At first I thought this was a terrible idea, but Mark's certainty grew the more he learned. After we decided to look for crew, I found myself unexpectedly weeping with relief. I had no idea how much the offshore plan had been stressing me out. Offshore sailing was a hurdle that we could face later, when Mark had more experience.

Now we were reaching Beaufort, and the time for passage-making was coming close. Yet thirty- to fifty-knot fronts were sailing over us with alarming rapidity. We had a crew plan, but it was not happening the way we'd hoped either. Mark's faithful instructor friend from his trip-leading days, who'd wanted for years to sail with us, was recovering from appendicitis. Another guy had fallen in love, and his priorities had changed overnight. A family friend, Ryan—bold, adventurous, and only seventeen—was on his way. But he was young and inexperienced, and there was only one of him.

We reached Beaufort one day in late October, without having sailed through the night on the outside ocean. It was the end of the first leg of our journey. What would happen next? We anchored in a river that flowed by the town and searched for libraries and parks. We bought the girls sandals and told stories of white sand beaches. But inside, things were churning. Every morning Mark checked the forecast. His comments betrayed his unease. "The wind is not supposed to get under thirty knots for five days!"

Now that I wasn't going, I had become the cheering section. "It'll calm down enough for you to get across the Gulf Stream—it always does," I said. Soon I would be seeing my new nephew while we waited out the voyage in Philadelphia. I figured Mark and Ryan could handle it somehow.

Ryan arrived at a nearby airport, and Mark borrowed a car to pick him up. Ryan was a young idealist, a solar/wind power consultant, a small sailboat owner, a sail shop veteran, a homeschooled learner, a somewhere-between-boy-and-man with his own priorities and dreams. He was a perfect fit for us. Being one of seven children, he was prepared to share. As I showed him around the cabin, I became acutely aware of how completely we lived on top of each other. In fact, once we stepped off the stairs, there was really nowhere else to go. Ryan would be sleeping with his head just inches from the toilet, and just a couple of feet away from us. I looked at him with a question in my eyes as he took this in.

He nodded quietly. "Looks good."

In a few hours, he had figured out how to get out of the way, and within a few days his stuff gradually integrated into our space until it all but disappeared.

Our first night together, the cabin felt too cramped for five. We ate supper out in the dark, windy cockpit. Mark hung a little candle lantern above the cockpit table and everyone found a place. I passed up the chicken and potatoes and the girls chortled with joy.

"I can tell you had a car, Mom, to have chicken and potatoes!" Cedar said.

Ryan was quiet. Having flown the red-eye across the country, he was ready for bed. I prayed that the girls would show mercy in the middle of the night, a time they were prone to fussing.

Ryan at the helm.

The next day after breakfast Mark asked Ryan, who had grown up off the grid, to look around the boat and help him with the solar panels. By lunchtime we were given the welcome news that the solar panels had never been properly hooked up and now we had twice the juice we'd ever had! We cheered when Ryan came downstairs for lunch. He smiled. He was, we were learning, a quiet guy.

A couple of days later, with a potential favorable forecast looming for Mark and Ryan to leave on the big passage, we rented a car to drive to Philadelphia. But first we went grocery shopping and filled the dinghy with fresh produce. The girls hugged Mark tightly.

"Have fun, Daddy!"

Then Mark and I turned to each other. "Don't forget to eat the vegetables," I said lamely. Were we doing the right thing? Suddenly nothing seemed certain. We were never the types to be apart. A tight hug, and the girls and I climbed up to the car. I drove timidly at fifty-five miles per hour and hugged the right lane. Had fifty-five always been this fast? We were off to Philadelphia and adventures of our own.

Back in Beaufort, front after front came through. A group of sailboats set out, then slunk back into the harbor two days later with repairs needed. We talked on the phone daily. Tension wracked Mark's voice as he tried to decide what was the right thing to do and whether it was responsible, or whether he was ready, to head out on a passage that would almost certainly bring them into storm-force winds.

Finally, one morning a week after we'd left, he called me. Another extremely marginal weather window had come and gone, and the season for leaving was disappearing. "We aren't going," he said. His voice cracked. "I really need you to support me in this."

On the other end of the line, I was silent. Finally I murmured, "Whatever you decide is fine with me."

I knew this was not what he needed, but it was the best I could do. My faith in Mark was shaken, and it was my own fault. My trust in his total competency had blinded me to the fact that he came by all his experience honestly—by knowing how to avoid getting in over his head. His decision not to head out was demoralizing, rather than reassuring, to me. I simply could not imagine not doing what we'd said we'd be doing, no matter how facts, reason, and judgment pushed us in another direction.

"So, what next?" I finally said.

He cleared his throat. "Well, we're going to head offshore right now and maybe get as far as Florida." He probably felt me cringe right through the phone, because he rushed on. "Most families we know are headed to the Bahamas this winter—remember, our Plan B?" I cringed again. Mark always made up Plans B and even C, but I'd never considered actually using them.

We made it through the phone call, but after that contact was sparse. Mark and Ryan were offshore, heading down to Florida. I told my sister Lamar that we weren't going to meet up in the Virgin Islands after all, but would meet instead in Georgia or Florida and then head for the Bahamas.

"Well—*phew!*" she said. "Am I allowed to be terribly relieved?"

Relieved? I had not considered that she might be concerned. I decided there was a measure of comfort in taking the safe option. The Bahamas might not be exotic and remote, but I knew they would be manageable. When I talked to Mark a few days later, his voice was clear again. He'd completed a three-day offshore passage and was feeling good.

"Mom, when are we going back?" Cedar asked every day. She was going to preschool, but the excitement had worn off and it was time to resume her normal life.

"I miss Daddy," Lamar reflected every night in her bed. "We are not really a family right now."

I missed him, too. Even aside from the difficulties of single parenting. I kept feeling confused, as though I'd discovered an arm missing. I just wasn't fully there.

Finally, after thirteen days of separation, we flew to the Georgia/Florida border. We raced through the airport and came flying down the escalator. At the bottom stood Mark, open arms and a huge smile overwhelming his usual reserve. The girls flew straight into his arms, and so did I.

The girls chatted loudly over each other in the car, each eager to tell Daddy the most stories. Mark and I could barely get a word in edgewise, but we smiled at each other a lot. We scrambled out of the dinghy onto the decks of *Amicus* and raced down into the cabin, the girls squealing as if they'd been away for years.

"Ryan!!!—are you there?"

Ryan put down the book he'd been reading and stood up with a smile. In minutes he was holding the girls upside-down, as they shrieked with delight. I watched as I contentedly cooked the first decent meals the guys had had in weeks. I tossed the moldy vegetables without a word of reproach and found apples, cabbage, carrots, raisins, walnuts, and mayonnaise to make a crunchy "salad." Dinner was joyous and in Lamar's prayers that night she voiced her satisfaction: "Me-play-Ryan-all-day-Amen."

Soon the days settled, and we resumed our regular rhythm. Ryan opted to continue with us down the Florida coastline. We wanted to head out into the ocean, but the weather refused to accommodate us. Oh well. Mark and I were so glad to be reunited that the issue of how, where, and when to take off every day receded. "Without my family, I'm just another schmuck on the waterway," he told me.

I smiled and leaned in for another long-missed, tight familiar hug. We had learned numerous lessons in this process of changing plans, not the least of which was that we needed to tread very carefully when talking about it. Almost without knowing it, we could carelessly ride roughshod over one another's most vulnerable selves.

Until this point, we had always avoided the roles of captain and crew on board. We thought an equal partnership meant equal decision-making in all things. But the truth was, we were *not* equal on *Amicus*. Mark had the sailing skills and the responsibility. He was the captain! No matter how much I wanted to go somewhere, if he wasn't comfortable with it, we couldn't safely go there. When I envisioned a good "crew," I suddenly saw how I needed to be: unquestioning and cheerful. At times, I could offer an opinion. At other times, not. In an edgy situation, what a captain needs is a crew that instantly supports what needs to be done. Only when Mark felt that complete support could he make decisions with confidence. Only when he was confident could he venture out of familiar territory. When he felt trusted, he wanted my opinion. As our trip evolved, Mark grew more confident and I grew more mature, and we breathed a sigh of relief when that particular type of storm faded into the more distant past. Sometimes, when we can't solve a problem, we can instead outlive it.

I grew up in the Swedenborgian faith,[1] which means among other things that we figure ourselves to be eternal partners—through this life and beyond it to the next. Living a good life together gives us the chance to experience "conjugial love"—a love between soulmates that gives them "innocence, peace, tranquility, inmost friendship, complete trust, a mutual desire of the mind and heart to do the other every good."[2] This is a love that does not disappear with death, but continues in the spiritual world. So we had lots of time to figure it out. I knew Mark was my guy, and he had always felt instinctively that we should never, really, be separated. We always figured that when we meet up again in the spiritual world, having presumably left this world at different times, I would find him contentedly prepping a sailboat, waiting for my arrival. His welcoming words would be, "Shall I fire up the diesel, honey?"

While we felt new tensions in our marriage on the water, we could not help but appreciate that sailing provided us with the best opportunity we knew to cultivate these "conjugial" states with and for each other in our daily, minute moments. Was Mark feeling innocence, peace, and tranquility when, in the middle of the night, we heard a rat in the cockpit and he instantly went out to chase it away with a bucket of water? No, but his longing to protect his family and home was palpable to me, every day. I witnessed and appreciated every helping hand he gave his fellow sailors. And every hug, encouraging smile, and seasick effort I made to read the girls a few more lines from a storybook or swallow another cracker, he knew I was doing for him and for the vision of our life. It was no different from what many parents experience together, but our mutually agreed-upon dream simplified things. The job to be done was crystal clear. There was no one else to distract or rescue us.

Ultimately, it was not *Amicus*, nor the weather, nor the itinerary, nor the children, that would make or break our sailing trip. It was us—Mark and me. Our partnership was immediate and constant, flowing intimately through the flavor of our journey on the water. Daily, we confronted the hard, glorious fact that we could give each other and our children the most precious of all gifts—our presence, our attention, and our unlimited time. We bore witness to each other's struggles, and also to one another's bliss. When I burnt the rice, Mark not only ate without complaint, but cleaned the pot without a word of reproach. This was a man who, when I was pregnant and could not abide another day in a windowless bathroom, cut a hole in our bathroom wall and installed a window during a March blizzard. His dedication to my often-whimsical needs enabled me to trust him enough to go on this adventure in the first place—something I never would have conceived of on my own. Turns out, what we were capable of giving one another was really far greater than I had guessed. One day I found myself watching him struggle with the ropes while the wind whipped his hair and aged his face—and saw that I loved him more than I was capable of loving him before this all began.

Notes

[1]Members of the New Church—Christian organizations based on the writings of Emanuel Swedenborg, an eighteenth-century theologian, scientist, and visionary whose thirty-five printed volumes open up spiritual meanings in the Bible. "All religion is about life, and the life of religion is to do good."
[2]Emanuel Swedenborg, Conjugial Love no. 180.

Chapter Twelve

Florida

Right before Thanksgiving, we crossed into Florida. On Thanksgiving Day, *Amicus* was docked next to a boatyard where several couples were repairing their boats. In a fit of optimism, I bought the smallest turkey I could find, ignoring the strange look Mark gave me. The oven shrank before my eyes as I brought the turkey into the cabin. Although the turkey was twice as big as our oven, it fit nicely after I cut off the legs, wings, and thighs, then cut what was left in half. My "turkey" was done in two hours, and we cooked the rest of it separately. Against all odds, it tasted delicious. We feasted on a potluck lunch with other cruisers. "How did you cook a real turkey?" asked our new friends. I was happy.

But after Thanksgiving my outlook darkened. Florida had never crossed my vision as a voyaging destination. Florida was a way of getting south, like Nebraska is a way of getting out west. To make matters worse, our national commercial culture was ushering in the Christmas season. "Let's at least try to be game about this," Mark suggested.

The girls pulled me grudgingly along to a Christmas parade. Trucks drove by covered in colored lights and filled with kids throwing candy at us. I waved my arms vigorously to reject the tosses before they came. The girls were well versed in the evils of high fructose corn syrup but still enjoyed having things thrown at them. Cedar announced, "We will take anything that is *protein* or *things*!" No one took her up on her offer, but she held to her position for the entire parade, undaunted.

We were saved by Bunny, a former cruiser who spotted us anchored in a lagoon out her condominium window. She met up with us on a sidewalk in front of her door and inquired after our boat. Eager to talk to someone other than ourselves, we were soon engaged. She became our chauffeur, dinner hostess, tour guide, grandma, and cruising advisor. We stayed in her sphere for two nights and two days. The girls showered her with hugs and kisses when we left her.

By the time we were within striking distance of Fort Lauderdale—a popular taking-off point for the Bahamas—sailing was no fun, and after a while we stopped hoisting the sails at all. Bridges came up fast and furious, and the channel narrowed. Heat, bugs, and endless waves of pink townhouse skyscrapers were wearing down our resolve to live with gratitude. One evening, Mark commented, "It could be worse." He pointed to a sailboat one hundred yards away that had run aground in low tide. The sailor sat in the cockpit waiting for the tide to go up, right in front of a bar at happy hour. A row of gawkers enjoyed his predicament. I didn't.

I did count my blessings after we rented a car and became *de facto* landlubbers for a few hours. After a long and rushed series of shopping ventures through endless strip malls, Mark manfully offered to drive Lamar and Cedar through the mess to a drugstore so Cedar could purchase a set of dice which she had earned by going an entire week of nights without fussing. While they shopped, I returned home in the dinghy and cooked supper.

They didn't get back until after dark. I waited for them on the curb of a busy four-lane road. When Mark pulled over, I grabbed the girls and shoved them into their lifejackets. With cars whizzing by us at sixty miles per hour, they hopped into the dinghy. They practiced their rowing skills with me in the waters nearby while Mark parked the car. It took the whole evening for our blood pressure to fall back to normal. This was a normal life to some—but not for us! It was unbelievable how much noise and tension could be packed into a single day. Mark was right—it could be worse.

Heading south once more, we passed through conglomerate superstructures that gave hints of humanity but defied our standard definitions. Were they towns? Cities? Suburbs? We saw high rises, real

Killing time.

estate offices, boutiques, spas, saloons, and a townhouse for sale for $1.8 million. But where were the groceries? The one deli we found was fully Spanish-speaking, employees and customers. Two worlds lived side by side—the service providers, and the property owners.

Eight bridges later, we found a little "lake" in Ft. Lauderdale, surrounded by estates. This was our stopping place. From here, we planned to head out to the Bahamas. But we weren't leaving any time soon. The winds were blowing twenty to thirty knots out of the north into the indefinite future.

One afternoon, I overcame lethargy and perpetual-motion fatigue and went for a run. As I jogged along Mercedes Lane, I kept an eye out for places we could land our dinghy without being kicked off by a butler in a mansion or a deckhand for a yacht. As I ran, I pondered the absurdity of our country's wealth distribution—or lack thereof. But as the service providers, all people of color, watched me jog by, I suddenly realized that we were not that different from the cruiser-yacht owner. We, too, were on a joyride enjoying the luxury of life on the water. A greater gulf separated us from the workers who sat at the bus stops, who scrubbed the decks and the bathrooms, who had never owned a dinghy large or small and who were much more concerned about the next paycheck than about landing ashore to play on the beach.

I returned to Mark and the girls at our pre-determined spot by a bridge. Mark rowed his arms off to bring the dinghy up to me in thirty knots of wind, while the girls sat straight as arrows in their lifejackets. They ducked, screaming and giggling, under a bridge. They didn't care or even notice whether we were in Fort Lauderdale or the Bahamas—or China, for that matter. Their distance vision was a blur. Their focus was right in front of their noses. They had it right! What

Making tortillas with the clothes wringer.

mattered right now was jumping in water, ducking under bridges, swinging from masts, chatting with people, eating yummy food, and sleeping well.

Northerly winds, squalls, thunder, and lightning plagued us. I struggled to learn or relearn patience, humility, and humor in a small space. I was more in the mood to emulate the magnificent qualities of Strength and Endurance—Shackleton-style.[1] What was this adventure about, anyway? Often, success meant simply keeping my mouth shut and keeping my crabbiness from spilling out over everyone. I received but miniscule reward for heroic effort, and I got little credit. Once Cedar told me, "Mom, I think you need a time out. You're ruining everyone's day."

Great, I thought, fully immersed in self-pity. *I can't even have a bad mood without souring the whole family.*

A disconcerting rumor that we were only allowed to stay on this lake for twenty-four hours, as per city ordinance, underpinned our eagerness to leave. However, word among cruisers, and confirmed by a recent court case in Florida, was that waterways—including our lake—were federal public property, and it was illegal to kick traveling cruisers out of them. At the heart of the issue was the unspoken sentiment that local property owners didn't like riff-raff anchoring in their backyards, discharging their dirty water, and occasionally leaving derelict boats to rot.

We weren't going to abandon our boat, or discharge any sewage. We were simply stuck by the weather. After hearing different sides of the issue, we decided not to try to solve it but simply to survive it. We couldn't afford to tie up in a marina. We were desperately trying to leave. We would just do the best we could. As it turned out, the "best we could" meant a stay of over two weeks.

After ten days, we still had not been harassed or kicked out by the police. Police ticketed our friends for speeding their dinghy (while a motorboat zoomed by) and told them to leave the anchorage in twenty-four hours. Another couple was ticketed and told to leave, but since they were waiting for a new engine, they stayed put. Mark called the Seven

Seas Cruising Association for advice. They told us to keep a low profile. We also didn't have the city's required green/red light for nighttime travel on the water, so we didn't dare use the dinghy after dark.

Finally, things started looking up. We heard that critical "S" in the forecast. The Gulf Stream runs south-north, and we were not about to question the wisdom of avoiding a cross wind-current situation at all costs. Southerly winds wouldn't arrive for five days, but it gave us hope. We befriended a docked yacht owner who let us land our dinghy at his dock, giving us access to the beach and playground. We took a bus downtown and happened upon a bilingual, multi-cultural library program, led by a Spanish-speaking dynamo who had songs and books for four December holidays.

As the time of possible departure drew closer, our nerves frayed easily. One morning I took the girls shopping. Rowing for the first bridge, I was lost in reverie until Lamar asked me, "Will we fit, Mom?"

The tide was high, and the current was sweeping us under the bridge with less than three feet of clearance.

"Duck!" I shouted.

Instantly the girls dove low, yelling for the echo as we slid under the bridge. When we had climbed up onto the dinghy dock, we tossed our lifejackets back into the boat, but the wind caught one of them and lifted it into the water.

"Back in, girls!" I hollered, and we jumped back in. Cedar untied us and we rowed furiously to our lifejacket that was floating away.

"What a day!" she commented happily.

We visited the library and the grocery store. Walking back to the dinghy, we were tired. I had the girls in the jogger, and they were eating yogurt. When they finished, I tossed the empty plastic cups into a nearby dumpster attached to a townhouse. A thin, suited woman with short blond hair walked briskly by.

"We pay for that!" she scolded. I gaped at her and considered tossing the yogurt cups in the street, then controlled myself. We moved on.

Meanwhile, back on *Amicus*, Mark was having his own adventures. The first thing he did after we left was to pull out the v-berth cushion and lay it on the cabintop to dry after a bed-wetting incident the night before. Then he turned on the engine for the first time in a week, only to find the water pump spurting liquid. He dug out his spare pump, read the directions, and replaced it. Disaster averted. He stepped outside and noted immediately that the v-berth cushion had flipped into the water in a gust of wind and was out of sight. He was without a dinghy, but he wasted no time.

"Hey! Hey!" he hollered around until he had attracted the attention of the nearest boater, who came over in a dinghy. They motored to the shore and found the cushion, just in time to see us returning from town.

That afternoon, disaster struck again. Mark was out in the dinghy and the rest of us were napping when I heard a loud *honk*! The police had returned, and they meant business. They were writing things down.

"Knife River, Minnesota," (reading our stern) followed by an expletive, which did not incline me to greet them.

I sat down on the settee inside. "Girls, sit here with me."

They did.

"Mom, are we hiding from the police?" Cedar asked.

I looked at her. "Sort of. Well, yes."

We listened to them circling us. Our dinghy was gone and it looked like we were all away. They went off to harass other boats. We heard loud confrontations, followed by engines turning on. Boats were leaving, their crews fuming in the cockpit. I cuddled the girls and wept with relief. I could not have handled a confrontation without Mark. When Mark returned, we headed upriver and downtown to the cheapest marina we could find. We were tired of feeling hunted, and we needed to find some energy reserves for the biggest passage of our lives thus far.

As our desperation to leave mounted, so did our anxiety about being tested as sailors again. There was nothing so demoralizing for us as going long waiting periods without sailing. Just as a great day on the water opened up our horizons and left us feeling like seasoned

The night before departure.

sailors ready to conquer the world, long waits and motoring left us hanging our heads like little kids, barely fit to venture off the anchor. We gradually came to accept these extremes as par for the course, taking them for the cyclical feelings they were. We couldn't help but wonder if we were up to the task at hand. But finally, we were going to find out.

The silver lining during this difficult time came while I was crossing a busy highway a few days before. We ran into another family with a jogger. They came from the same direction as us. We started talking and realized we were both heading across the Gulf Stream. The Teskeys's boat's name was *Satisfaction*. Their boys—Connor and Dylan—were just younger than our girls, and Dylan had cerebral palsy. We were instantly enamored. Julie, the mom, and I took about three seconds to get acquainted. Kerry, the dad, and Mark were instantly comfortable. Mutual need drew us together like magnets, and we started planning our departure together. Another family we'd met in the Chesapeake also swung into Ft. Lauderdale, this one with three girls. Instantly we dinghied over and hopped on board.

"How's the schooling going?" I asked Jennifer, the mother.

"Terrible," she answered.

I grinned. Another mom ready to talk! Within hours we were also planning to depart together.

So we would not be alone as the final night drew near! Three families banded together, leaving in staggered starts due to our varying boat speeds. The end was in sight. I just hoped our main sail wasn't full of rat holes.

As the slowest boat, we left first in the late afternoon on December 23. We navigated the narrow channels leading out to the ocean, successfully crossed under some major highways, found the proper buoys at the inlet, and then—just like that—everything improved. The wind was southerly, the waves lapped the boat, the sun was setting behind us, and a blessed silence engulfed us. I welcomed the queasy sensation that was far preferable to the low-grade headache that had plagued me in Ft. Lauderdale. We gathered a dozen picture books to read in the cockpit by the dying sunlight. Just before starting in, I looked up and gave Mark a huge smile. He returned it and even rubbed my shoulders. The girls cuddled in.

"Read!" We were back in the game.

Note

[1]Ernest Shackleton and his men, in one of the greatest feats of our century, survived a winter stranded in the Antarctic, a trip across the deadliest sea in the world in small sailboats, and an unsupported, unfed trek across a mountain range.

Leaving Florida.

Chapter Thirteen

The Bahamas

Our passage across the Gulf Stream was smooth and manageable, and by mid-morning the next day we found ourselves at a resort on Grand Bahama Island, the traditional spot from which to start a cruise in the Bahamas. The weather was hot and sunny, the water was crystal-clear, and the sand beaches were white.

"Mom, look! Neighbors!" Cedar chortled. She watched through the porthole as Kerry biked up to us, kids in tow in a cart behind him.

"You guys up for a trip to the beach?"

Already the girls were dashing for their bathing suits.

In the afternoon, we remembered that it was Christmas Eve and thought about decorations. Back in Florida, we had glued together a wise men mobile which was almost destroyed before its hanging because Cedar wanted to keep her *own* wise man separate. We pulled it out again and, with true Christmas spirit, Cedar allowed the wise men to stick together. We wound lights around our wood stove and pulled out our Christmas picture books. The girls put up their stockings and fell into bed. Mark looked groggily at charts while I wrapped a few presents. We turned in early.

It was a glorious Christmas. Appreciation for small pleasures was in the air. Just being out of Florida was enough for me. Cedar's big gift was Candyland, and Lamar's was scissors. She could hardly put them down. Soon the cabin floor was littered with paper triangles. In the mid-afternoon, we gathered with other cruisers on the beach for

The morning after crossing the Gulf Stream.

food and storytelling. Julie Teskey told us their story of losing their boat on a reef on Lake Ontario and driving down the coast to find a new boat. Dylan, sitting in her lap, grinned from ear to ear as she remarked, "It's not how far you fall, it's how high you bounce back, eh?" Our mouths dropped in admiration of their courage and grit.

By the end of the day, the Christmas lights around the stove were in the way. Off they came. Other than little bags of beef jerky and yogurt raisins that had filled the girls' stockings, all signs of Christmas quickly disappeared. Easy on, easy off. We played Candyland all evening. Lamar had just figured out the concept of the game, and she participated with a flourish of pride and joy. Cedar always won, because she was the only one who cared.

* * *

Christmas with friends.

A week later, in a calm twilight, we were coming into another anchorage. The stars were just starting to twinkle. Mark dropped the anchor with its customary *clank*. At that moment, one of the engine alarms went off. Mark dashed down to check it out, calling up to me to rev the engine. When I did, the alarm stopped. I thought this remarkably clever of Mark and hoped that was all there was to it. But ten minutes later, the anchor secured and the engine off, he gave me an ominous look before pulling off the hatch steps and peering down to check the oil dipstick—which came up empty. In a few minutes he turned to me. "The oil pipe is corroded and needs to be replaced," he told me.

"How did you know what the problem was?" I asked in awe.

"Because there was oil all over the place," he answered shortly.

On the bright side, we were not alone. Anchored nearby were *Satisfaction* and *Spoony*, the families we'd been with ever since crossing the Gulf Stream. Mark lost no time in spreading the burden—he immediately contacted Kerry, who came over to provide eyes and commentary as they peered into the engine together. Mark from *Spoony* brought over extra oil.

The next morning, in a dead calm, these two families took turns towing us past many lovely islands. Not only did we travel faster than we normally did, we even cleaned house while Julie and Kerry took our children for almost an hour. With undistracted energy, we emptied and cleaned out the composting toilet, washed the kids' quilt, and took showers in the cockpit with our black solar bag of water.

At that point, Kerry radioed us that our reprieve was about to end. They slowed down and we glided up to them. A smiling and unperturbed Julie held a sobbing Lamar at the bow, ready for a quick handover. We heard a chorus of howls from the cabin, presumably Cedar and Connor quarrelling. Kerry and Julie assured us that the chaos didn't bother them. So we took Lamar and let Cedar stay, wondering if she had finally met her match. She was returned to us later, subdued but cheerful.

At dusk, we were finally "let go" from our towline and drifted into an anchorage tucked up next to Green Turtle Cay, a village that boasted a commercial enterprise capable of ordering parts. The next morning, Mark ordered a part through George, who owned a shop. George was a big guy with dusty blond hair. He worked mostly for cruising sailors whose engines were broken down. He'd moved to the island years before to slow down his pace of life, and he wasn't about to be rushed. When Mark asked him for a rough timeline for getting the part, he scratched his head and leaned against a chair in his yard. "Oh, maybe about a week."

For "island time," that wasn't bad at all, and we settled in to wait.

We'd heard that the local kids came out on Saturday nights to play games on the street and eat French fries and ice cream. This sounded excellent! We swam until dusk at a nearby beach, ate a pot of rice, frozen peas, and falafel, then headed into town where some younger kids had assembled on the basketball court. They casually

Hiking with the Teskeys.

accepted our presence and paid us no mind. They were busy tossing a basketball back and forth, shouting to each other with great enjoyment but no clear rules. Our girls avidly observed, holding tight to our hands. When a ball wandered our way, Cedar grabbed it.

"Go ahead, you can play," I encouraged. She hastily tossed the ball away. We bought ice cream cones and watched the older kids coming out to shoot hoops. It was getting late so we left and found our way home.

Rowing back to *Amicus* in the pitch blackness, Cedar said, "I think they were nice."

Bright and early on the day we'd calculated that our part would arrive, Mark arrived at George's. George said the part might still be in Florida, and if it was, it could arrive later that week.

Several days later, Mark stopped by again. Still no part. Should he come by later? Naw, George said, he would bring it by when it came.

No problem. We breathed deeply and said goodbye to *Spoony* and *Satisfaction,* who were moving on. The wind started blowing hard, making it less likely that George would travel to another island to pick up the part. I was restless, not adjusting well to the lack of forward motion. One hot, sticky day, I told Mark crossly, "I don't care what culture this is. Please find out when we might expect that part."

Mark disagreed. "He's doing his best. We shouldn't bug him." Several days later, we found out that the part still needed to be brought across the Sea of Abaco. I stopped holding my breath.

Saturday night rolled around again. This time, two little girls approached us shyly, and Cedar happily facilitated the introductions. It didn't take long for the universal kid-language of giggling, chasing, and shouting to take over. The teenagers arrived and got into the act—shooting hoops, performing cartwheels, leaping off picnic tables, and doing back-flips off chain-linked fences. Who needed a playground? Lamar was still on my lap, her shyness losing the battle to her almost overwhelming urge to join the fun. Suddenly she burst out of my lap and dashed across the court to retrieve a lone basketball. She picked it up and started racing back to us. Just short of her destination, her eyes skirted the court. She veered off, passed us right by, and instead tossed the ball to a kind-looking child. She chortled with joy and returned to my lap to strategize her next move.

We ate ice cream and picked up two bags of trash. The local kids helped out. One little girl asked, "Are you going to pay us for doing this?"

I laughed. "We're just cleaning up. Who wants glass in their hands from doing handsprings?" We left dusty, tired, and at peace.

During the third week, we heard that George was heading off the island to pick up a bunch of ordered parts. Lucky for us, but unlucky for anyone who needed to visit his shop that day. No matter what George did, he was letting someone down. Now I felt generous. *Good for him*, I thought, *meandering along at his own pace, unimpressed*

123

Beach time.

by every cruiser's urgent engine troubles. He could provide valuable consultation to all us modern consumers headed on a crash course toward heart failure and high blood pressure.

Bright and early the next morning, Mark took the dinghy over to George's shop. An hour later, he slid by with another guy in another dinghy. "We see the parts," he called, "but we need to ask George before we take them."

Shortly after, someone came by to report that Mark and George were headed to the bank to use the credit card. Another good sign! By late morning, Mark was back with the part and several spares, too.

We switched into high gear. Lamar and I did one day's worth of food shopping, which was all we usually did since stores had fridges and we did not. We then confined ourselves to the cockpit while Mark sweated below. In a couple hours, after running the engine for a few tense minutes, he pronounced us back in business. The tube he'd replaced fell apart in his hands. We could have ruined the engine—and missed all that fun.

Green Turtle Cay, where we'd gotten the engine repaired, was a great place for travelers. But other places were not. We arrived at Marsh Harbor expecting a real "destination," largely due to its popularity and the size of the town. Hundreds of boats anchored there, many of them parked for the season. We arrived in early February. Cedar and I explored the town twice in two days—once hastily, then exhaustively. Both times we came up empty. Main Street traffic was hurried and without sidewalks. There were no playgrounds except one tree on a drab lot with three iffy swings hanging precariously—which we did try. The shopping center had all the charm of a chain store back home. We knocked tentatively on the library door, and those inside told us it was closed. The used bookstore had only trashy novels and no kids' books. Cedar eventually found a street corner with some grass where she could throw wood chips into a puddle without being run over. We spent time in town watching a native boatman cracking conch shells, digging out the conch for restaurants, and occasionally sneaking in a bite for himself.

For four days we couldn't leave *Amicus* at all due to the strong winds. A dinghy ride would be dangerous, and Mark and I kept an anchor watch around the clock in case we dragged. Inside the cabin the motion was bouncy enough that I felt too woozy to cook real meals, or color, or read. We slept only lightly. Entertainment was at a low ebb. I spent a lot of time in the cockpit. The girls emerged every few hours to take a look around.

"It's hot and seasick inside," they commented. They took a romp around the cabintop and retreated below. I sat there and imagined the mess being created inside.

We often found ourselves in survival mode after extended periods like this, until something indescribable would shift and our energies would begin to exist in harmony again. When I finally went below, everyone had staked a claim on a cushion and was in personal

Snorkeling.

space. The girls were "reading" their books, their quiet murmurings intended only for the dollies. By mid-afternoon, the wind had lessened and we were relieved from anchor watch. We all snoozed heavily. By suppertime, balance was restored.

Once the wind settled down, its direction kept us from leaving Marsh Harbor. We turned our attention to snorkeling.

Cedar had received a snorkeling set for her birthday, but lacked the coordination to breathe underwater through her nose while floating head-down. Until one day when she got it! It was a nautical rite of passage, like learning to ride a bike. She floated, head down, for forty-five minutes. Mark floated along with her. I couldn't tell who was more delighted. Exclamations bubbled up through Cedar's snorkel every few seconds. When they finally emerged, she was shaking with cold but could not stop raving about the world she'd discovered below the surface.

After we snorkeled ourselves into oblivion, Mark focused his attention on a problem that had plagued us since the start of our trip—nighttime bugs. All the coming into and going out of the hatches made full-proof de-bugging impossible, and we'd not had a bite-free night yet. In the Bahamas the no-see-ums ruled. We purchased the finest screen we could find and covered all the hatches and portholes. At dusk, we shut ourselves in and gleefully watched the buggers surround the boat—until Mark, reading to the girls in the v-berth, looked up at a critical moment. The front hatch screen was just inches from his face, which allowed him to watch a no-see-um crawl right through the screen and fly onto some nearby skin. Our quiet bedtime routine was interrupted. Chaos ensued, all fresh air was shut out for the night, and I despaired of sleeping peacefully ever again.

The next day, Mark remembered that he had one final defense against the bugs—a mesh tent he had used for sleeping outside in northern Minnesota and Canada, where mosquitoes and black flies covered a tent so thickly they provided a low static hum all night. With nothing but time to kill, he dove deep into the bins under the v-berth, uprooting the entire area like a mole making a home. He emerged with the tent. The mesh, he correctly remembered, was so fine it was like a silky sheen. Instead of trying to keep the bugs out, we would just try to keep the girls in. He hung the tent inside the v-berth, and at bedtime the girls dove under. He pinned the tent under them and declared there would be no getting up to pee at night until further notice. It worked! The girls slept quietly.

Some places were easier to enjoy than others, but every place we visited was valuable. It was in the less desirable destinations that we learned resourcefulness, gratitude for small pleasures, and the great lifelong lesson of acceptance. It helped to stop questioning our trip every time I was in a place I did not want to be. After all, most people do not question their decision to live on land after a bad week.

One day on a long, wet dinghy ride, we donned raincoats, crouched low to avoid the splashes over the bow, and played word games. Lamar's favorite game was called "favorites." "What's your favorite breakfast?" was the first question.

Cleaning.

"My favorite healthy breakfast is eggs or grits," answered Cedar, pointedly omitting oats, "and my favorite unhealthy breakfast is pancakes and French toast."

I thought, with disbelief, that we once had wondered, *Can we survive together on a boat?* The question had evolved to, *Can we live on land again?* At times like these, the simple challenges of self-entertainment, cheerful pitching-in, and the endurance of temporary miseries felt much more manageable than the challenges that faced every landbound family. I could read a storybook one hundred times and return to it with a smile, but could I face a thirty-mile commute with similar grace? At that moment, I didn't know.

Chapter Fourteen

Making Decisions

I have never liked turning around. When I go for a run in the early morning, I always have to persuade myself to turn around. I want to peek around the next bend. I want to use myself up. I'm feeling good. As soon as I do turn around, I usually wish I'd done it sooner. I can't enjoy the ride back because there's always a time crunch and I have to hurry. Or, I'm more tired than I felt coming out. Or, I'm bored. The adventure is over. You'd think I'd learn when the proper time to turn around is, but I never do.

Two months after leaving Florida, we arrived in Georgetown. As anyone who has cruised the Bahamas knows, Georgetown is the hub of the wheel. Hundreds of cruisers are drawn there, whether by social need or by the necessity of getting groceries. On its popular daily radio net, cruising socialites offered support groups, financial advice, weather conferences, volleyball tournaments, happy hour, and lost and found. Georgetown for us was like alcohol to an insecure teenager—we didn't really approve, but we didn't have the confidence to say no, either. We couldn't deny the benefits of all the company—especially all the children reported to live there for the winter on their boats. We were curious how this would affect our family. We didn't think we needed daily or weekly activities that resembled those of a retirement community—we were pretty sure this wasn't what cruising was about for us—but we hadn't had a grilled hamburger on a beach since we'd left home. Maybe, we reasoned, we weren't Georgetown types, but we needed groceries badly. It wouldn't hurt to take a look.

We arrived to find hundreds of sailboats and a few power cruisers sitting placidly just feet from each other over a two-mile beach. We sailed slowly through the crowded inner city and landed somewhere in the near suburbs. Our anchorage was not in immediate danger of being invaded, but the possibility was definitely there. We dropped the anchor and turned on the radio. In a few hours, we found ourselves getting sucked in. We heard about kiddie events and forgot that our kids had survived just fine without kiddie events for the last six months. Family Regatta Week—an annual festival by and (mostly) for cruising families that included boat races, kid activities, and lots of (pricey) food—was coming up and signs were everywhere.

On the first day we dinghied over. We pulled up to a beach, nudged our dinghy in with dozens of others, and walked over to the action, feeling shy. I remembered that I never was a partier. The girls slipped their hands into ours as the noise increased. We sat the girls at craft tables. Cedar dived right in, though she checked to make sure one of us was behind her every few minutes. Lamar just watched. We didn't see anyone familiar.

After lunch we meandered over to the big event—a miniature sailboat race. Every participating child had created a boat, and its mettle was to be tested in a race. With great fanfare, kids prepared their boats. Some sunk just seconds after launching. Others tripped along mightily to the finish line. A great roar arose when the winning boat crossed. Its owner, a teenage boy who'd lived for many winters in Georgetown, proudly displayed his craft.

"ARRGGG" came a growl from right behind us. We jumped. A pirate with black teeth, a hook for a hand, and a leering grin peered over our shoulders. Lamar shrieked and Cedar grabbed Mark. But the pirate had already moved on. He was painting blood-red scars onto kids. I asked the girls, "Do you want him to paint you?" They looked at me in horror.

We wandered far from the pirate until the girls' grips on our hands lessened. Cedar turned her attention elsewhere. "Daddy, can we have some candy?" Soon both girls were tired and whining. Mark and I looked at each other. It was time for a quick exit.

Watching the kids' boat race in Georgetown.

When we first arrived in Georgetown, we moved to a different anchorage every time the wind changed. We watched hundreds of bobbing boats and wondered aloud why everyone wasn't like us. But anchor dragging was rare. After a week we found ourselves staying put more often, too. The feeling that company was precious faded. We played with the friends we'd met before arriving but we had less in common with the families planted there for the winter. They seemed bent on entertaining themselves. Where was the interest in experiencing local (non-tourist) culture, or venturing farther into the Caribbean and places beyond? We didn't play beach volleyball or drink, and we were all about getting away from people like us.

My birthday arrived. I was focused on talking to my family in the U.S. Hoping for a minute on a satellite phone, I waited in line at a pastel-green shack that served as a cyberspace connector, satellite connector, and convenience store. I watched tanned cruisers stare at their computers while local kids raced around snatching cans of Vienna sausage from the sagging shelves while their mother—the storekeeper—chased them around and threatened with a stick. She nursed her baby, then handed it over to an old man to hold while she sold mac and cheese, condensed milk, and canned ham at the cash register. Everyone was glistening with sweat. Dogs came and went, sniffing and gulping the sausage remains. I wanted those Vienna sausages, but something held me back. I got a few minutes on the satellite phone before the connection was lost.

Instead, I found my way to the big supermarket. Fresh foods had just arrived. Cooking and eating three delicious meals in one day was the best birthday present I could imagine. I bought vegetables, grapefruit, and mango. I brought back actual ice to the boat, giddy with excitement. The girls were just as thrilled as I was, and I chipped off enough ice for four large glasses of ice water. We drank lustily.

With three sisters to call, I was not ready to give up on the phone call yet, so I hustled over to a friend who owned a satellite phone. I ran out of gas on our little dinghy's outboard motor—which we'd acquired from sympathetic cruising friends—but rowed home for more. Still, I couldn't make the connection on the phone. My friend gave me a longer cord and suggested phoning closer to the antennae that was up on a hill. I took the phone to a dock, plugged it in, and stared intently at the antennae as I made the call. No luck.

In the afternoon, I radioed Julie Teskey, floating in *Satisfaction* one-hundred feet away. "What are you up to?" I asked.

Her voice came back over the air waves, crackling comfortably. "Our dinghy deflated last night. Kerry's reviving the outboard." She paused. "Hey, Happy Birthday! You two should go out to dinner!"

So it was arranged. The girls would have pizza on *Satisfaction*. Mark and I dinghied into town. Aside from the conch shacks that closed at dinnertime, our only option was a hotel, overpriced and touristy. We squirmed in overstuffed chairs and were served delicate portions of fish that were probably shipped from Miami. Mark said it first. "This isn't exactly the dream, is it?"

I snorted. "I don't know when I've felt so out of place." It was a great relief to speak and hear those words.

We mused and vented together, tentatively stepping onto new territory. We discussed the things we love about sailing, something we hadn't done for a long time. "What I really love is pristine shoreline," I mused.

Mark added, "With a little topography behind it."

"And seasonal change," I couldn't help but add. We looked at each other and laughed.

"You do know what we've just described, don't you?" Mark said with a wry grin. "Lake Superior."

When we walked away, I felt freed, empowered. We were not, in fact, trapped into any plan or any place. We could choose our destiny.

The next day, we retreated from the social scene and found a short path leading to the quiet ocean. There we entered into a virtual retreat that lasted several days. Each day we hiked there, let the kids loose on the beach with instructions to entertain themselves safely until further notice, and sat ourselves down to talk, listen, figure, and plan.

Something was shifting. Finally, we were ready to look our situation straight in the eye. Suddenly we had lots to say to each other. Our feelings about the Bahamas took some time to unravel. On the one hand, it was a pleasant way to spend a winter—and a marvelous break from the headaches of Florida. We appreciated the safety of the Bahamas and the endless beaches of which our kids never tired. On the other hand, we were underwhelmed with certain aspects of the "cruising life." As rich—we could no longer deny this label—white foreigners surrounded by other cruisers, we weren't experiencing meaningful interactions with the Bahamian people. We knew we did not aspire to a perpetual vacation. We were bored. We still wanted to show our daughters the world and to contribute meaningfully to it. But how? Was cruising the answer for us?

Somewhere in there, we granted each other permission to question. A waterfall of doubts—shocking and refreshing—began to pour

Decisions.

out. Who said the Bahamas were so blissful? On the other hand, were we really ready to live in countries where we had no knowledge of the native language? We wanted to discover pockets of still-untouched coastline and meet "average" people surviving and thriving without tourism. But many barriers were keeping us from traveling farther away. Mark had more, and bigger, questions, about heading into the far corners of the big oceans than he did when we first set out. I was pretty sure we could live as nomads for a while longer, but I wasn't sure I wanted to. Once we started talking, we couldn't stop, and we ducked under this virtual waterfall every day for a week, just to feel the drenching wetness again and see if there was anything more we could say. We weren't exactly searching for answers, but the mud began to clear.

As the hurricane season approached, our choices were twofold. We could head southeast, into the wind and toward South America, or we could return north to the United States. The southeast route was well known to be a long and arduous battle against headwinds, and our ketch was not made for sailing into headwinds. Even if we could get down to South America in time, we weren't ready to commit to living in non-English-speaking, developing countries for over a year. But the alternative filled us with a sense of loss, shame, and failure. If one was not ready to go south, one must go north. So it seemed we were making the decision to return to the United States, just as we were starting to breathe easy from getting away. No wonder it took us a week of meandering to come to this dreadful conclusion!

Once we spoke this realization aloud, we stared at each other as shock, disappointment, despair, and giddy relief tossed through us. It took us a couple days to realize that we were still good people, and possibly even adventurous ones. Slowly, we began to get used to the idea of returning. What we would do once we were back in home waters was a topic we left alone, having finally learned not to plan too far in advance. Our new plan was humble and manageable: to get out of Georgetown, do some sailing, and see how it felt to be "turning around." We left Georgetown the next morning and headed for a nearby cluster of islands.

Why is it that goals once reached, shrink? In my deepest feelings of failure, I could barely recall the triumph we felt when we sailed away with four aboard for the first time. Reaching the Atlantic, crossing the Gulf Stream—none of those accomplishments had disappeared. So how could it be that we were sitting in the southern corner of the Bahamas, feeling like we hadn't done a thing? If we were depending on a never-ending string of greater and greater goals for our sense of worthiness, it would backfire on us sooner or later. Here it was, happening right now. We could stop this pattern.

Any act that limited possibilities—that burned bridges—was empowering by definition. It created motion. The decision to turn around propelled us on a path. Before then, we were paralyzed at the junction without even knowing it. We had no idea how much this former plan of ours was bogging us down until we let it go. Afterward, the spring came back to our step, and we felt as light as our light-air sail.

But our decision-making wasn't over—in fact, it had just begun. After a week or two of cruising in islands south of Georgetown, we felt compelled to discuss its implications. Should we sail the East Coast for a year? Move to land? Where? Quickly overwhelmed by these big questions, we decided to simply leave those questions unanswered. But this was not easy for either of us. Soon we were locked in a cycle of satisfaction/confidence that would swing to panic/despair. In an effort to both accept and escape from our mood swings, we made a decision to refrain from any discussion of our future. What had started as productive envisioning was turning into an indulgence, a way to escape the present. The mental skills that "turning around" exercised were decidedly rusty. It was time to sit silently, to pray individually, and to wait for the mud to clear.

After only two days of silence, we had a moment of truth. I was lying in the v-berth and letting the tears flow, as they tended to do, silently and for unknown reasons. Mark poked his head in and said, "Let's just go back to Minnesota. Make that the given."

He returned to the girls in the cabin. I stopped crying and lay silently, listening to my heart and to his. Somehow, he needed to say the word. When he did, and I had permission to return to Minnesota, I knew immediately that's what I wanted to do—so badly that I hadn't even dared voice it. I snuffled, got up feeling like a petulant child, and came out of hiding.

"Okay."

So, once again we made a Plan. It was so simple it might actually work. We needed to regroup, and to do so, we were going home. It might not have sounded like a very exciting plan to some, but for me it changed everything. I was never meant to be a nomad, I realized with some surprise. Adventuring was all well and good, as long as it had a beginning and an end. Just as Mark was the expander in our partnership, I was the contractor. He had provided us with wings. I would now inspire in him the blessings of a deepening root system.

Waiting for the mud to clear.

Returning home was not an admission of our failure to sustain ourselves on *Amicus*, but an acknowledgement of the blessings we knew on land: earth and climate that fit our bodies, work that was fulfilling and filled a niche, people and culture that matched our souls. Some never find this in a lifetime.

So . . . northbound! In the contrary way of the Providential Wind, we came to this realization right on the cusp of a most unusual week of northwesterly winds—great for heading to the Caribbean, impossible for those bound for the US. We were itching to go, but no physics in the world could move *Amicus* north when the wind and waves were blowing her south. Still, we were not deterred. We knew now that living in the present was by far the most pleasant way to live. It was time for Mark and me to take as full advantage of today as our girls took every day of their lives.

Chapter Fifteen

Education

The next afternoon, the sun and the clouds were particularly beautiful—crisp white floated against a deep-blue backdrop, every shade of turquoise, green, and white in the water below. We packed a lunch and loaded ourselves into the dinghy.

We had nothing but time and looked at the island with new, interested eyes. We nosed into an estuary and took the dinghy as far

Monument to Columbus/Lucayan Indians.

up as it would go. At the end, we landed and put both girls on our backs. Without another human in sight, we headed up a long dirt road to the northern tip of the island. The excursion brought us refreshing land-variety challenges: blistered feet and sore shoulders. Ahhhh, this felt good! I stretched my tired shoulders and did a little yoga. At the top of white cliffs, with swells crashing into brilliant white breakers hundreds of feet below, we found a simple stone monument dedicated both to the peaceful Lucayan natives, and to the landing of Columbus. We grimaced at the irony, since very soon after Columbus landed the Spanish exterminated the Lucayan Indians. But in that majestic setting, I could accept the paradoxes of life, and appreciate both the centuries of simple Lucayan life on this remote and lovely island, and the incredible feat that landing here from the Old World certainly was.

Throughout our stay in the Bahamas we'd been eager to learn its history and culture. We were intrigued by what we observed. The islands did not appear to have a simple economic system, political history, or ethnic population. Their very complexity became their signature identity. After disease and the Spanish massacre killed the Lucayan natives, the islands lay uninhabited for almost a century. Much later, English Loyalists escaped to the Bahamas from the American colonies before and after the American Revolution. Slaves of revolutionaries who had escaped (and were "freed" by the British) also sought refuge here. The Loyalists tried and failed southern-style plantations, but their British leanings and culture continue to influence Bahamian culture. Some left, abandoning their slaves, who farmed crops friendlier to the tropical climate. Piracy was common during the 1800s. By 1900 the idea of traveling to the Bahamas for pleasure took hold, but hurricanes flattened homes and discouraged population growth. Boating, fishing, and beachcombing remain popular today, with most native Bahamians involved in tourism of some kind.

Unfortunately, the crystal clarity of waters in the Bahamian bank is deceiving. The Bahamas suffer the same global contamination and development that we see everywhere else. Up in the Abacos Islands, we had discovered an estate owned by a man in Florida. While building a row of three-story weekend townhouses for wealthy foreigners, he declined to buy the expensive but environmentally safe waste-removal system, instead opting for the cheapest, waste-goes-into-the-water system. The Bahamian government, according to a fellow cruiser, signed his permit without a peep. In another case, a small, international environmental group called Reef Relief faced off with businesses and locals over conch-fishing regulations. The businesses won, and conch-fishing habits that endanger the long-term health of the coral reefs, and ultimately the tourist and fishing economy of the Bahamas, remain the status quo. As we observed these battles, we wondered if our own perspective on the environment would change if our immediate livelihoods were at stake.

Initially, it seemed that garbage and decrepit buildings simply didn't bother the Bahamian people. Then one day it dawned on me that most of the mess was hurricane damage. The empty lots and piles of concrete were not forgotten or useless real estate, but homes that had been suddenly abandoned or destroyed. Garbage, not carelessly littered but blown in by storms, haunted the otherwise pristine shorelines—plastic containers half-full of sand, a potted plant, a huge cement door, a hanger suspended under a mangrove branch. Most depressing was the paper-thin layer of plastic—often in shreds, or bleached by the sun, but nevertheless fully intact—that enshrouded many beaches almost invisibly, washed ashore from some distant land or ship.

Some beaches showed hints of the future as well as the past in the rough trails that marked new property lines. Soon three-million-dollar-per-lot houses seemed destined to cover many of the islands.

"I think we're seeing the last of the 'old' Bahamas," Mark commented one day.

Poverty and excess ran side-by-side, parallel streams that rarely flowed into one another. As the girls and I searched futilely for a playground or anywhere that children could play, Mark talked to a cruise ship owner whose vessel boasted four floors, five televisions, and four full-time staff—all for a boat used one or two weeks a year.

Most Bahamians we talked to considered their government the biggest source of corruption and exploitation. It was selling all their real estate to foreign developers. At the same time, they seemed light and carefree, unconcerned about their future. Would this optimism translate into determination to preserve Bahamian culture—its natural beauty and sunny diverse population? I hoped so.

One day, after waiting at a rumored bus stop without success, we decided to try hitchhiking. With this simple decision, our time in the Bahamas was transformed. Our thumbs were barely out when a car, driving by on the dusty, narrow road, pulled over. The driver took us about halfway to our destination. Then we waited for a full two minutes while several cars and golf carts passed, drivers waving and shouting explanations about why they couldn't pick us up. Apparently their sense of collective responsibility necessitated a good excuse to pass us by.

We rode the second half of our trip in an old truck full of bottled water. The driver was a young man with a big smile. With a sweep of his hand he pushed aside all the stuff in the seat beside him. We squeezed in and the girls climbed onto our laps. We asked about the island.

Gesturing grandly, the driver proclaimed, "The peace and quiet, yah, this is what makes the islands." He and his wife had grown tired of the city of Nassau's violence, crowds, and rush. They moved down here to slow down, work, feed the kids, and live more simply. He started selling bottled water and juice. He was getting what he wanted, and that's what he loved about the islands.

"Yah, these islands will be exactly what you make of them."

By the time we reached our destination, we knew the truth: the islands would be what we made of them.

Five minutes later, we were walking along a lone road. "Hey!" I shouted. "Where's our backpack?"

Mark slapped his forehead. Our backpack was still in the back of the driver's truck, with our radio, digital camera, and all our raingear. We didn't even know the guy's name, nor he ours. I looked at Mark. He shrugged. We were thinking the same thing. The islands would be what we made of them, right? We weren't going to be worriers. When Cedar asked about our stuff, I responded hazily, "Oh, we'll figure it out."

Collecting water for our tanks.

Later that afternoon, as we walked back along the lone road that led back to our boat, the driver took a detour off his route, found us, and returned the backpack.

As he waved his arm out the window and his truck disappeared around the sandy bend, we started walking again. The girls swung between Mark and me. We lifted them high into the air. If we could just hold on to this trust in the process of our journey, surely it would all be okay. In fact, it already was okay. What a glorious day!

We soon learned that hitchhiking was the easiest way to make inroads physically and socially. How could we have missed this before? There were other tricks, too. We learned not to follow crowds, but to listen intently when experienced travelers with similar priorities shared information. We learned a lot about finding food. With little ground soil and a close proximity to the United States, most food in the Bahamas was imported. Prices were approximately twice what they were in the States, and the imported produce was set off in the corners of the stores. Much of it was rotten.

What did the Bahamians eat? I was mystified. At one island group, the only "grocery" store was a convenience store by the gas pump at the dock, and all the cruisers complained about the lack of fresh food. One day we caught sight of a man with peppers and tomatoes on a boat. We sidled up to him and asked where the fresh food was. He directed us to a big grocery store at the other end of the island, offering to give us a ride.

On the way home from the grocery, we were soaked by a rainstorm—an unusual treat in the Bahamas, where every day was beautiful and seasons brought only slight changes. As we meandered down the narrow road we heard the sound of brakes screeching. Minutes later we passed the scene of the accident: a golf cart had hit a car. Those involved were immersed in a benign, business-like conversation. Did people here just work things out when there was an accident? It stood to reason. We were learning that usually cars were owned, or at least used, collectively. Many locals drove with their doors open (an invitation for others to hop in), or they used motored golf carts instead of cars. It was in everyone's best interest to manage the car/cart population on the island in a friendly way to keep those doors open.

As we tripped over chickens in the street and watched young children driving carts and cars, I couldn't help but wonder if many of the United States' regulatory laws were really necessary. Why shouldn't people be capable of regulating themselves in their day-to-day lives and neighborhoods? The police certainly did not seem overburdened with policing here in the Bahamas—the police station was a bright pink house covered with Christmas lights.

One day on Long Island at the far end of the Bahamas, we ran into a young Finnish sailor who had sailed from Europe on a boat made of flattened beer kegs. We peered inside his cabin and exclaimed admiringly. We shook hands with four deckhands, roughened young men and women who looked like they hadn't showered for a long time. One was eating a can of beans. They nodded and smiled.

From there we hitchhiked twenty miles to the next town. On the way, we plied our friendly driver with our usual questions. How did people eat here? He told us what we'd suspected but never seen: many people grew vegetables and kept chickens, goats, and lambs. He said you could always buy fresh, local food if you knew where and when to go. "On the family island, you are safe," he told us proudly. "People are here to be away from the city." Later he said, "This island is the cleanest of all the islands.

It did feel clean. Long Island nurtured its own culture, and the independence was palpable. The prices were more reasonable, with the food geared to regular people rather than tourists. We ate a greasy, cheap lunch and followed it up with a rich, locally famous dessert called *guava duff*. We waited in line for our food for a long time, yet nobody was outraged or apologetic. We found a church on top of a hill where we'd heard one could climb the steeple. No one was around, but the door was unlocked. "Just go on in!" the townsfolk encouraged us.

So we did, carefully climbing a series of narrow, rickety ladders. In the Unites States, this area would have been fortified with safety devices and warning signs, or blocked off altogether. But here, we took care on our own and were rewarded with a rich view of the harbor's brilliant colors. Afterwards we stuck out our thumbs for about ten minutes before a long yellow station wagon drove slowly toward us and then predictably came to a stop in front of us. We peered in the window where an aging man with deep smile-wrinkles waved us in. Right away I knew we'd found someone special. He told us about his family, his life as a preacher, his take on world politics, his former life in Jamaica. He'd even been to Egypt.

"Where are you headed?" he asked us finally. When we told him he nodded.

"But you can drop us off wherever you need to," Cedar piped up.

"Oh—I passed my house a long time ago," he answered. "'If a man asks you to go a mile, go with him two.'"[1] It was a reference to his source of truth—the Bible—and I felt wistful as we got out of the car and said good-bye. My own experience with such deep contentment was fleeting enough that I longed to learn the secrets of those who lived it every day.

Altogether that day, we had covered architecture, economics, social studies, environmentally sustainable practices, physical education, religious studies, nutrition, and motor mechanics.

"Do you think our kids are getting an education?" I asked Mark. He laughed.

* * *

It was spring. Easter loomed like a blank slate—no expectations, no traditions, no fancy food. We were newly humbled with the decision

Exploring a shipwrecked plane.

to turn back. We had said goodbye to most of our friends. We felt alone among crowds. We were unsure of our immediate direction. We were tired. We were open to seeing beautiful things in strangers. In short, we were emotionally used up and empty—the right mental state in which to be filled.

Having anchored near a small town, we took the dinghy up on Good Friday for a church service, but due to tidal currents and some swells coming in from the ocean, we couldn't get closer than a couple miles to town. Trusting in local good will, we got on land and started walking. Within five minutes, we got a ride and arrived at the service, soaked and sandy, with two minutes to spare.

Instantly, I was glad we made the effort. The simple church building, with windows wide open to the breeze, was half full, but what the congregation lacked in numbers, it made up for with zeal and

Easter egg painting.

vocal talent. The theme was praise and celebration—two things in which we were in short supply. The energy crackled, and we absorbed it like food for the empty soul. When the crowd finally swept outside, we shook hands and exchanged wide smiles. From there we were sent, hips swaying and feet tapping, on our way into the Glory of God. Mark was a master on the dinghy ride back—nothing like the disciples in the Gospel who were fainthearted in a storm. Mark had direct and immediate knowledge that the Lord was right there with him. The current swirled with eddies and pockets, but Mark headed into the whirling dervish and brought us through it straight and true. We crouched inside to avoid splashes.

Easter dawned beautiful and calm. We read the Easter story from beginning to end.[2] We were struck by its raw and rich immensity—its encapsulation of despair, betrayal, endurance, trust, triumph, and transformation. We understood Jesus' sense of betrayal, the impossibility but necessity of the task at hand, the power of letting go. I felt Mary Magdalene's unwavering devotion, her despair and misery, her disbelief in a world that was not what she thought it was, and the euphoria of possibility. I thought of all we'd gained—and lost—in the past year. I could relate. We really do need to lose our lives to find them.[3]

Easter didn't change our situation. We were still unsure of ourselves and without nearby friends. But the sharp edge of our depression had softened. We were not alone. The islanders had reminded us that there are many meaningful ways to live. Most importantly, we felt the gentle, unjudgmental presence and love of God—a feeling that did not disappear after the holiday ended. Having thoroughly enjoyed every holiday we'd experienced on board, we concluded that tradition can be beautiful and meaningful—but something is lost when it comes ready-made.

* * *

After four months of beaches and small towns, we approached the city of Nassau in late spring. A police boat motored up to us as we came

Pure fun.

Even more fun.

zipping up a crowded channel in a squall. We were thrown into a panic. Was there paperwork? Were we in the wrong lane? How could they consider stopping us with a squall bearing down? The driver cracked a smile: "Is everything all right?"

We laughed with relief, waving them on.

Remembering our city skills, we took a bus downtown. The courthouse sat beside the library, and while playing hide-and-seek, Lamar and Cedar brushed disinterestedly against a man in handcuffs who was chatting jovially with his police escort. We'd often noticed policemen engaged in conversation with their charges. Sometimes it was even heated. In the United States, you get out of the way if a policeman and a civilian are shouting. But then, these policemen came from pink offices.

Notes

[1]From the Bible: Matt 5: 41
[2]Bible verses: Matt 26-28.
[3]Matt 10:39 "He that finds his life shall lose it: and he that loses his life for my sake shall find it."

Chapter Sixteen

Back Across the Gulf Stream

HISSSSS . . . I looked behind me. I was poised in the cockpit, alone. A full moon was rising at our stern, and I could see easily. We were rollicking along in steep eight-foot waves in the middle of the night and the middle of the Gulf Stream. The winds were coming from the same direction as the current—mostly—but still, the waves were lumpy and irregular. They looked scary to me, and I turned forward again and listened to them hiss as they broiled under the hull. The crest of a wave broke over my back, shocking me out of my stupor.

We'd been in bigger seas, but not at night in the Gulf Stream. Rolling was normal. But not like this. We were *rolling*. It was rockus, and it was loud. *Amicus* was a "wet" boat, meaning she took in water easily, and let it go easily. In waves like this, water regularly washed in over the stanchions. The entire deck was wet on both sides, often inches deep. All portholes and hatches were closed. Inside, everything rattled, shook, or leaned. The cabin was filled with new sounds.

I willed my shoulders to drop and checked the compass. We were doing fine. After the first 10,000 or so waves, I began to breathe again and glance behind me. The wind vane was magnificently silhouetted as we rollicked up and down—now against the moon's shadow, now against the moon. How I loved that wind vane. She was the third adult every couple knows they need—quiet, steady, unobtrusive, and generous. With a simple set-up of ropes in the cockpit, we could attach her to the tiller in any decent breeze and let her sail the boat. She took our most stressful job away and left us with four free hands. In these conditions, she was in her element.

Behind her, the whitecaps caught the moonlight and glistened. There was no land, boats, or buoys in sight. It felt as remote and wild as anything I'd ever experienced—more than a canoe trip in the northwest territories, more than a silent night in northern Minnesota listening to a wolf howl, more than the top of a 12,000-foot peak in the Rocky mountains in a hailstorm. This was distant, and immediate. Dark, but glimmering. Peaceful, but loud. The part of me that yearned to become one with the earth began to breathe. Could it be that I was saturated? I found myself thinking, *This is enough*.

I also felt absolutely convinced that the only way we were going to survive the night was in the palm of God's hand. We were too tiny to have any say in the matter whatsoever. At first this felt terrifying. But as the night wore on, I could feel myself wrapped right there in God's hand. Maybe the trust we were putting in ourselves, our boat, and ultimately the Divine, was worth rewards like these.

In the wee hours, the wind and seas moderated. Our fitful sleeping deepened. This was "regular" rolling, stuff we were used to. Mark took over in the night and by morning we were through the Gulf Stream.

The girls woke up and immediately came outside. They were cheerful because they knew what to expect for breakfast—cold cereal and hot chocolate. With a sidelong glance at Mark, I crept away to kiss *Amicus*'s hull and caress her sides. As often happened after a rough period, I felt convinced that her lively spirit had carried us lesser beings through the valley of the shadow of death. We owed her everything.

Then I set about making breakfast and setting the cushions and lee cloths back, grateful that the cabin held together so well in the dark chaos of a rolling night.

Amicus was not luxurious, but she was more than special to us. The farther we strayed from civilization, the better she served us. Because of her, we were able to experience life as it was meant to be lived. Common sense, skilled hands, and a pulse on the subtleties of the earth's messages were the most important traits we could master. Of all the gifts *Amicus* offered us, this was perhaps the most precious.

I came out of the cabin with the requisite cold cereal and hot chocolate. The girls fell upon their breakfasts. I squinted up at Mark. "Your oats will be ready in a minute."

He nodded, gazing ahead. I followed his eyes. The air was hazy. Hazy! We'd hadn't seen anything but blue sky, puffy clouds, and gray storm fronts for four months. Condominiums and high rises were visible through the haze. We'd left this sight with such relief just four months before. But the familiarity was surprisingly comforting. Buoys to mark the way. Rules that we understood. "It's amazing how one's perspective can change," was all I said to Mark before diving below for his oats.

I dropped a handful of gorp on the oats, sprinkled cinnamon on top, and handed the bowl outside. The girls had left their cereal and were leaning over the lifelines, crowing with delight. Dolphins welcomed us back, and birds soared overhead. Why weren't there any birds in the Bahamas? Even the thick brown water was pleasantly familiar.

We motored up the ICW in northern Florida for a day before anchoring. The next morning, we headed straight to the customs office to check in. Our customs official was brisk with us, especially after Mark (scrupulously honest—and also aware that the military had every inlet on camera) told him that we'd come into the ICW the morning before. One is supposed to check in within twenty-four hours. We were given the "Consequences of Failure to Report" to read. Mark studiously pulled out his reading glasses to read the report while I tried to control my irrepressible eye-rolling. Eventually we all realized that the boat (or the anchor, to be precise) did not actually Touch American Soil until 7:00 the night before, well within twenty-four hours of the present moment. The situation improved. We left as free Americans. All we had to do was go online to pay for the privilege of checking in and for all the expenses incurred.

Next, a park—one with a slide and swings and intact monkey bars. We marveled at the public restrooms, the free ice water spouting generously from the public drinking fountain, the sidewalks empty of litter. We appreciated the unknown people and policies that were providing all this for us. We walked to a grocery store and gleefully filled the shopping cart. The girls ran through the aisles screaming "ORANGES!" "BANANAS!"

I hustled behind them and avoided eye contact with other shoppers. Was it so bad to appreciate food? I ogled the kale with an absurd lust and put a big bunch in the cart.

"I'll carry it if it doesn't fit," I told Mark who was eyeing the backpack. He managed to cram it all in, though, and hiked all the food back to the boat while the girls and I meandered to the library. We ate yogurt on the steps before going in. In the late afternoon, we put the girls on our shoulders and headed back to the water.

We found a used book store and spent forty-two dollars—a rare splurge, but what a gold mine! Reading the books we had onboard had lost its appeal. The girls didn't want to hear the only books I would consent to read. Cedar's Little House books were in such tatters that she couldn't pull them out without leaving a trail of paper shreds on the floor. Now Cedar, hugging three new, unread Little House books, was actually speechless.

At the park by the harbor, we were astonished to see people helping themselves to strawberry fondue, chicken wings, and artichoke dip while a live band played nearby. It was a Chamber of Commerce fair, with food for anyone. Trying to act civilized, we piled our tiny plates with food. We felt like distant acquaintances of a wedding party as we eyed the crowds and minded our manners. It cemented my opinion of this town—Cocoa Beach, Florida—as one of abundance, generosity, and positive endeavor.

Back on the boat, I dropped a big chunk of square ice into the icebox and carefully stored yogurt, milk, and cheese in beside it. The icebox had served merely as storage space for months. I had known plenty of hot, moldy moments in those four months. I learned how long a carrot lasted at eighty degrees. I was tired of cooking three meals a day from scratch. But eventually, I had allowed the food challenge to take us in the direction we wanted to go anyway—towards health, whole foods, and simplicity. Now that we were back, ice was an unspeakable luxury.

Back on the ICW, the weather was hot and muggy, and the tides were very low. One humid, windless day, we pulled into a creek near a small city. Boater traffic was heavy, and I hated relying on the engine after four months of sailing. I was not one bit surprised when the engine flaunted its power over us once again by sputtering and dying. Mark dashed to the front and dropped the anchor, which left us in the middle of the channel—safe, but conspicuous. In minutes, Mark popped up from the engine compartment looking sheepish. Our first tank had run out of fuel. Okay, I had to admit, that one wasn't the engine's fault.

He switched tanks, pulled up the anchor, and we were off— when the engine sputtered again. Even I knew what needed to be done when there was a potential air bubble in the fuel lines—bleed them. Mark was wet with sweat, pulling up heavy chain and working deep in the hot engine. The girls emerged from the v-berth where they'd been explaining the current emergency to their large dolly family.

"Daddy, can we go fishing?" They knew no fishing was allowed when the engine was running due to the danger of fouling the propeller. They dropped their ropes over the lifelines and waited dutifully. Twice Mark bled the lines, and twice more the engine sputtered. I leaned over his sweaty shoulders. With the engine exposed, we could neither enter the cabin nor get near the galley. I tapped him on the back. "Hey, we're going to need food."

Mark stepped aside and took a much-needed water break while I fixed a quick lunch of burritos, carrots, and apples. I offered graham crackers but Cedar told me, "Graham crackers aren't a treat anymore. I'm going off them for a while."

"Not me," said Lamar, reaching for Cedar's crackers with a sidelong glance to me. Cedar let her take them.

The third time the engine revved up, Mark pulled up the anchor. We motored up the channel. My eyes were glued to the depth sounder, which showed twenty feet, then four, under the keel.

"Uh—Mark!?" But it was too late. We were aground in thick mud, with no idea which way to go into deeper water.

Dolly naptime.

Numerous skiffs and powerboats passed us, and no one even gave us a wave, let alone an offer of help. I wondered if we were invisible, or just ridiculous. Mark hopped in the dinghy, poked the oar around in the water, and determined that we simply needed to go a few feet to the left. He dropped an anchor in, returned to *Amicus*, and pulled the anchor rope taut, then tauter. *Amicus* swung grudgingly around in the direction of the anchor, freeing herself.

Mark smiled a wry grin as we slowly moved forward. "Aren't we supposed to be done doing stuff like this by now?"

Anti-climatic as our groundings were so late in our trip, they kept happening. We came to expect them—a type of joke designed to keep us on our toes. One morning we woke as soon as it was light enough to see. The evening before we'd bumped along the bottom for half an hour during low tide, then been released before bedtime as the tide went up.

157

Low tide was coming again in the morning, and we wanted to be gone by then. But it was no use. Ten feet short of the channel, we went into the mud again. With a falling tide, Mark acted urgently. He grabbed the kedge anchor, attached it to a rope, and forcefully threw it out. He tried to reel it in half a dozen times while I gunned the engine forward, but the anchor never held fast enough to pull the boat forward under pressure. Then, to my surprise, he jumped in the water.

"What are you going to do?" I asked stupidly. It was still very early in the morning.

"Push."

Mark actually managed to rock the boat. Then he swam out to set the kedge anchor one more time. When that didn't work, he pulled the boom way out. Cedar emerged from sleep, cheerful and chatty.

"Want some help, Daddy?" She pushed on the boom to hold it over the water while Mark swung out there upside-down, looking for all the world like a dead-serious clown. Cedar and Lamar, who had also risen to take advantage of the early morning entertainment, howled with laughter. I gunned reverse as hard as I dared. No luck. We turned off the engine, sighed, and started our day. A couple of hours later, with breakfast eaten and parents calmer, the tide began to flow back in. We drifted free.

After a few weeks, running aground was no more noteworthy than burning the oats—an event barely worth mentioning as long as everyone responded properly.

"Daddy can fix anything," Lamar commented once with a smile of satisfaction born of absolute security.

Mark's strongest asset as a rescuer was simply that he assumed the problem could be fixed, and that one had to continue to work until it was. More often than not, this involved such basic skills as pushing—not pushing the right button, but actually using one's arms and legs for a healthy shove. Recently he had offered assistance to another grounded boat by hopping into the waist-deep water and even convincing the captain to do the same. Together, they'd gotten the small boat free. No, Mark definitely did not mind looking slightly ridiculous, or doing the dirty work, or acting fast. I could smell a burning breakfast or type a keyboard faster—but I had a slowpoke's rescue instincts. If the mast were falling, I'd probably be looking up and thinking, *Really? Oh, no!* while Mark would instantly calculate where we should go, yell what we should do, and possibly grab the right rope to lessen the impact.

One evening I was fiddling with the lid of the pressure cooker in which pinto beans were boiling rapidly. Somehow, Cedar tipped the pot and the boiling beans splashed all over her. I froze in shock. Mark—an EMT with unerring instincts—instantly grabbed a water bottle and poured cold water all over her body, calling out for more:

"Cold water! Cold water!"

After a second or two, he shouted over Cedar's screams, "Where are you burnt?"

Lamar with her cardboard digital camera.

159

"NOWHERE!" she hollered.

Lamar was also hysterical. I tried to calm the voice inside me that screamed half-forgotten tidbits of information from earlier days of first aid-training. ("Swelling-will-increase-over-six-to-twenty-four-hours-and-then-decrease!" "Blisters identify second-degree burns!") Instead of digging into the depths of my brain to access the relevance of these details, I took the simpler route. I cuddled them both, one on each knee while Mark took a solid look. Red splotches covered Cedar's inner thigh. Mark squirted out a dabble of aloe gel and prepared to lather it on.

"No!" screamed Cedar.

I took it from Mark and murmured sympathy while gently dabbing the spots. Cedar consented, more interested now. Mark got me the homeopathic remedy kit—a hundred tiny bottles of natural remedies—and I studied the books for a minute before selecting a remedy to treat her symptoms. Mark brought over a fan and plugged it in beside us. We watched for blisters, which never came. Mark gave a sigh of relief, pronouncing it a first-degree burn only.

"Okay, I need my knees back," I told Lamar, who reluctantly slid off but stayed scrunched at my side. "Did I ever tell you about when my sister Vera stuck her foot in a pot of boiling water on a backpacking trip in Wyoming?"

Smiles broke out. "Tell!" Cedar demanded. So I launched into every personal burn story I could think of, then branched out into all other childhood accidents. Mark turned to the beans and got supper going.

Mercifully, this accident occurred during the first cool weather we'd had in weeks. Instead of being restless from heat, Cedar snuggled under her blankets and slept deeply. Mark and I slept on a wet cushion—a minor inconvenience compared to what we could have faced that night. The mildness of Cedar's burn was no doubt due to Mark's brilliant water-throwing and the homeopathic remedy we'd given her.

This was the first and only real accident of our trip. It was a reminder to be grateful for our health and wellbeing, something we generally took for granted. Before our trip, the most frequently asked question we fielded was, "What will you do without a doctor?" This always mystified me. How dependent were we presumed to be on the medical world for our health? The decision to live aboard was a decision not to limit ourselves based on "what if's" of many kinds. Lots of things could go wrong on a voyage. *Amicus* could sink. Our bank could close. The country in which we were traveling could go to war. And, yes, we could need a doctor. This last, while not the least of our concerns, was never the greatest, either. Nowhere did homeopathic medicine provide better service than on the water, where a certain degree of self-reliance was essential and money was tight.

We had begun practicing homeopathy when we first became parents. After drifting through our young adult lives in health and invincibility, we were highly motivated to avoid hospitals, drugs, and tests for our children. It took awhile to shift our mentality from needing that quick fix (which drugs can often provide, at least temporarily) to acknowledging the body's own defenses and urging them on. But once the transition was made, a life independent of clinics and doctors became possible for us. We did appreciate what was available to us from the allopathic world in emergency care, pain relief, and serious injury, and brought a full-blown first aid kit—including heavy painkillers and antibiotics. We never used anything from it but bandaids and Tylenol, but we broke open the homeopathic kit often for everything from sunburn to bug bites.

Chapter Seventeen

Thoughts about Cruising

N ow that the end of the trip was in sight, we had time to think and ponder. Why were we returning to land? This was a sticky question. We could have referred to our financial limitations, but we knew others who found ways to finance a cruising lifestyle indefinitely. We could have harkened back to that pivotal

Hanging out on the Intracoastal Waterway.

conversation in the Bahamas when we realized that no cruising ground suited us better than Lake Superior. But we had the rest of our lives to sail Lake Superior. So there were other reasons. Mark and I talked about it one day.

"So why are we moving ashore?" I asked him as we sat in the cockpit. Lamar was on the cabintop holding a cardboard camera at arms length and taking "pictures" of herself. Cedar was sitting in the bow "reading" *Little House on the Prairie*. Each had a "squeegee" treat beside her—an overripe baby banana, opened at one end. Perfect for sucking. All was peaceful.

"I think I need a break from the worrying." Mark was very honest. "The truth is, things can always go wrong in an instant. Even if we try to escape, watch a movie on the laptop—I can never forget that if the anchor drags, we could be aground in about sixty seconds."

I nodded. "For me—I don't think I'm a true wanderer," I confessed. "I love our cruising friends. I love that the usual walls that keep

Quiet time at the bow.

Headstand while sailing.

people apart—careers, nationalities, family histories, economic status—disappear instantly with a shout across the water and a helping hand.

"But," I continued, "our timeline and agenda, like everyone else's, are unique. In the end, we are always on our own. I miss the next-door neighbor who will take care of my kids, attend their graduation parties, and send us flowers when our parents die. I miss doing these things for other people." I paused. "Also I feel aimless so much of the time. I'm not sure what my purpose is out here." At that moment, I felt I could not be happy indefinitely in the cruising lifestyle.

I wasn't sure I could be happy indefinitely on land, either. Sometimes when I watched the girls, I was afraid to move to shore. I had never accepted the mundane life considered normal for children in our culture. I dreaded car seats, rigid school days, and clean clothes. The media and advertising, sugar, bullies, and pollution, all provided me with plenty of fodder for worry. The longer we were on the water, the stronger was the girls' identity as liveaboards. Their cardboard cell phones turned into radios. Cedar walked around with a dangling thread attached to her finger, a mobile "telltale" so she could always tell where the wind was coming from. One morning, I was cooking breakfast and casually wondered why the boat was swaying side to side, when I heard, "Hey, mom!" I ducked outside and looked up. There she was at the top of the mast in her pjs. Mark was belaying her, a contented grin on his face.

One evening we headed into town for a celebratory dinner. Both girls were dressed to the hilt—the number and color of fabrics between them dizzied the eyes. We happened upon a restaurant with a bluegrass open mike night, and the musicians began to gather with guitars, fiddles, banjos, mandolins, and a bass. Jovial friendliness was in the air, feet were tapping, and harmonies were growing.

It was our sixth wedding anniversary. Through the noise I squinted at Mark and remarked, "I guess I've learned a few details about you since we married, but I gotta say, you're the guy I thought you were. And it's a good thing, too."

"Yeah," he responded. "Ditto."

Cedar at the top of the mast.

Dinner finished, we moved up front to watch. Cedar and Lamar got up and danced. The lead musician smiled down on them. "Would you come sing with us?"

They marched right up to the mike, which he lowered for them. Cedar's sweet, high voice trilled easily: "Do Lord, oh, do Lord, oh, do remember me." A roar of applause drowned out the next line. Lamar stood faithfully by, whispering the words and rocking her ink-stained dolly in the sling on her shoulder.

A few days later, Lamar and I walked over to a local preschool. Twenty two- to four-year-olds ran, slid, swung, screamed, and burned energy under the glazed eyes of two supervisors who leaned against the chain-link fence that surrounded them. Thumb in mouth, Lamar clung to me. I picked her up, and mutely we watched. Was this our future? In five minutes, the kids were swooped up into their classrooms, and we turned back to the familiarity and comfort of *Amicus* and the water.

That afternoon, we were motoring along the ICW. We were in an extremely fast tidal current at low tide, and suddenly we swirled sideways. Instantly I could feel that we were aground. It was naptime, but the nap part was not happening. Cedar and Lamar were busy lying down inside, singing, "The Old Gray Mare" at the top of their lungs. They didn't even notice the boat heeling way over, but gladly came up when I said they could watch the towing. With great efficiency, two Sea-Tow skiffs zipped in, took down our information, and attached us to them with a tow line. The mud was thick, and we were in very shallow water. Cedar took one look and dashed below, Lamar following. They emerged two minutes later, beaming, papers in hand.

"Tickets, Mom!" They leaned out to our rescuer. "Here are your tickets!"

The guy stopped what he was doing. With a big smile he leaned over.

"Thank you very much!" He politely accepted the mysterious "tickets" and doffed his hat.

As I watched Lamar leaning over into the skiff and shouting her thanks, I wondered, *Is this the same little girl who clung in my arms this morning?* Had her unique comfort zone spoiled her for life on land? Only time would tell us.

Spring turned into summer, or at least it felt that way to us. By May it was sweaty-hot. Transitions loomed. Mark made a phone call. By the end of the call, he had a job. He would be the director of a wilderness program along the north shore of Lake Superior in Minnesota. Doug (the same buddy who'd sailed with us to Isle Royale so long ago) and his wife, Lori, would be his new bosses. We breathed in the relief of knowing a paycheck was coming soon. Too soon, actually. Doug and Lori wanted him to start in a matter of weeks. This complicated our immediate future.

We decided to ship *Amicus* home to Lake Superior, giving us time to visit family on the drive to the Midwest and to get Mark off on the right foot with his new employer. With this decision, I felt a

Good-bye, *Amicus*.

familiar sinking of my pride. We were kow-towing to the priorities of the landlubbers before even getting off the boat.

Mark could read me like a book. "You know what?" He gave me his favorite line. "Life is too short. Let's just get over it."

So I let it go and we put our energy into getting the job done. It took us a few days to prepare *Amicus*, who I swear was grieving at the upcoming separation from us and the water. I wanted to embrace her and tell her how grateful I was that she brought us through so much so gracefully. I wanted to tell her that we would never let her down. She seemed to be coming undone. In one day, a toy bag broke off the wall, the cockpit table split down the middle, and our depth sounder told us nothing. I forgave her everything. If someone told me she was just a piece of metal with some ropes and wires attached, I think I would choose her over that person.

When I wasn't packing, I read books to the girls and made the daily meals while Mark prepared the masts for shipping. Soon we were hot, headachy, and depressed. *Amicus* sat at an expensive dock, exposed, flattened and wildly out of place. Her deck was naked, all sails and ropes and cushions stored away. The jogger, that precious carrier of girls, groceries, snorkeling gear, books, dolls, and thousands of gallons of water, was laid on the cabin floor. The masts lay sturdily over the cockpit. The icebox was open and empty. The girls chatted about their new car seats. Mark and I just sat. It was exactly one year since we'd first untied the lines from the dock and sailed eastward.

"I'm finding," I mentioned, "that getting on a boat is a lot easier than getting off it."

Unlike moving aboard, which took about two hours, moving to land took days. For one thing, we moved into a car first. We bought it right in the town where we left our boat and drove two thousand miles in three days. Sitting in the car made me stiff, a fact that intrigued me enough to do some calculations. On *Amicus*, we probably climbed the hatch steps at least four times an hour, seven days a week, for a total of about 35,000 times in the last year. No wonder this feeling of sitting still was so odd.

After a long day of driving, we walked into the home of Mark's sister and her family. Immediately, our nuclear shell broke wide open. Our life became a blur of hugs and guffaws, homemade chicken and corn on the cob, schedules and visits, and new bikes. The girls disappeared with their cousins, leaving Mark and me behind. We sat on the living room couch while everyone bustled around us.

"What do people do on land?" I asked Mark. He shook his head helplessly.

* * *

Sometimes, while we'd been sailing, well-wishers gave us a pep talk. "You're living the dream!" Probably we weren't glowing with euphoria or contentment the way they imagined we should. I was tempted to remind these people that they were probably living someone's dream as well—holding a steady job, raising a healthy child, not being shot at every day. Living a dream was still living. We were the same people on land or on water. We couldn't discover anything while voyaging that did not already exist inside us. Voyaging unquestionably had its moments of deep contentment and grueling anguish, but once it all settled in, we had the same capacity for anxiety as before and the same well of joy.

However, it was just potential until we left the dock. Only when we began living aboard did that part of us that was ready to live to the absolute fullest become actual. Our deep yearnings to live close to the earth, to be together, to raise our children in an alternative environment—all that became real as bugs bit us in the middle of the night, as we read stories while thousands of waves passed under us, as I grabbed a pot that started to slide off the stove in a gust, as we counted stars under the infinite night sky. Our minds were airlifted out of all the craziness of modern life—politics, cyberspace, traffic jams— and fixed where it counted the most: basic physical, emotional, social, and spiritual survival.

Since our trip, we have sought out others who choose a different path. Most of them are not on the water. They are farmers, homeschoolers, travelers, and random inspired individuals, couples and families who live amongst us without fanfare. But for us, *Amicus* was the vehicle that brought us into a life more aligned with our priorities. We had big dreams! We wanted to get off the beaten path. We also wanted to contribute, to find our niche of usefulness. Discovering how and when to nurture these ideas, or how they must be reined in, was and is our challenge. Just about everybody has dreams, but the actions that follow from them need not be set in stone. Life is not about maintaining an image. It is, rather, about watching the image transform, about allowing plans to ebb and flow like the tide. There really are no bad plans if we give them the best effort we can muster.

Back on Lake Superior.

Cedar at the helm.

Afterword

My hands closed around my stainless steel mug of tea. I had taken off my mittens to feel the warmth. I slipped one mitten back on, gripped the tiller, and gazed at the puffy white clouds and crisp blue sky above the bright-yellow shoreline of Lake Superior's north shore. It was early October, and the fall colors were at their height. Rock of Ages Lighthouse, which marked the southern tip of Isle Royale, slid by. We loved the National Park, and we'd enjoyed our month pushing the seasonal limit in our exploration of the northernmost islands of the Lake. But winter looked like it would arrive early, and we were lonely. We had not talked to anyone outside of our family for over two weeks. Cedar had an earache, and snow flurries were predicted for the next week. It was time to return to civilization.

Mark popped his head out of the hatch. "How are they doing in there?" I asked anxiously. Cedar, now seven, had an intermittent fever and the winds and waves were choppy.

"Fine." His face curved in anxiety, but his voice was firm. "Thirty-nine miles to go."

I said, "Well, we didn't ask if this would be an enjoyable trip. We asked if it was doable." And so far, it had been, with some luck. We were playing the odds. A gale was predicted, with winds right on the nose, starting sometime in the night. As long as it didn't come early, we would be all right. But we knew that no forecaster could guarantee anything on Lake Superior.

By dinnertime, we were within twenty miles of Grand Marais, our destination for the night. We could smell the barn. The girls poked their heads out to see a gorgeous sunset. After dinner, the motion picked up. I tried not to keep my eyes glued to the GPS, which told us if we were losing speed. Mark was a mask of concentration as he checked the charts, watched the winds, and considered sail adjustments. Eventually, there was no way to pretend that the winds were anything but dead on the nose.

He took all the sails down, and we motored determinedly forward. It was too bouncy to read. We threw up the lee cloths, pulled out the sleeping bags, and stuffed the girls in, one on each settee. Lamar, who had just turned five, had bounced around boisterously all day, entertaining Cedar, keeping herself warm, and helping me smile. Now she snuggled down, dolly cozily tucked in beside her. Mark and I said heartfelt prayers. The kids were more matter-of-fact: "Thanks for the wonderful day. Amen."

On Lake Superior.

I lay down between them and sang songs, as much to myself as to them. I vowed I would not look at the GPS until I was certain one more mile had passed. The unspoken reality was that the waves did not have to be that big to stop us cold.

By 8:00 p.m., we had less than ten miles left. One of us stayed inside, glued to the radar and the GPS—we didn't want to hit a certain treacherous rock in the vicinity. The other steered. I realized we were going to make it. The waves were not going to stop us. We were not going to freeze. The girls were sleeping soundly despite being airborne every few seconds. With a couple miles to go, Mark and I started to talk to one another. We were alone, out there in the black waters on the edge of freezing, every cell of our bodies immersed in the elements—yet we weren't alone, either.

It had been a little over two years since we'd moved ashore. The girls were vastly more capable and full of opinions. If we sailed to Greenland someday, they preferred pepper spray to guns as a protection against polar bears. Every year, sailing had gotten easier and more fun, and Mark and I looked at each other in wonder. Was it really payback time? Were all those seasick, overwhelmed, anxious days sailing with babies worth it? It was almost shocking to see things working out so beautifully.

Our transition to land, like our year on the water, was full of blessings and failed attempts. In most important areas, we scored. We found a home and a community that fed us deeply, and we settled in. Other elements of our new life—Mark's work, and the girls' school—seemed important at first. But over time, the pace of life and our inability to adjust to these benchmarks of modern infrastructure began to wear away at the things that sustained us—the biggest of these being time together. In bald fact, our year aboard had allowed us to do things that were somewhat unusual in modern life. Some of these were too precious to give up.

One day, I sat in my quiet house and listened to the roaring winds in the trees and felt ridiculously protected. Breakfast had come and gone before I even thought about the weather. It was time for a change.

Amicus II, June 2010.

One obvious problem was that we could only get out on the water for a week or two at a time. We needed to sail for longer than Mark's job allowed. We also wanted to test our abilities—and *Amicus*'s—for high-latitude sailing by staying out through a Lake Superior fall. So after two years of working and saving, Mark let himself go at his job, and the girls left school. We weren't against either, per se—but we didn't like the versions that were available to us, the kind that demanded our full conformity and commitment. We spent the fall sailing, then lived off the summer's wages and odd jobs for nearly a year while we searched for a bigger boat—one that would fulfill a new dream of taking others sailing with us, both for short stints on Lake Superior and full wilderness voyages.

Yes, our trip had changed us, indelibly and permanently. Perhaps the biggest shift was also the simplest—once we got back on the beaten track, it was much easier to slip off again. Our decision to turn around in the Bahamas had taught us that it must be okay to fail together. Crushing disappointment will eventually be followed by lightness and joy. We needn't be afraid of taking risks. We were free to choose our life. If everyone was doing something, that didn't mean we had to do it. If no one had tried this before, that didn't mean we couldn't do it. We weren't searching for bliss anymore—just contentment, endurance, trust during the rough times, and awareness of the flow of Providence, whose current is far more sustaining than the beaten path.

By the following spring we had our next boat. *Amicus II*, a forty-foot steel cutter, waited for us on the northeast shore of Lake Ontario. We sailed it back during the month of May and by June we were officially taking people sailing. Our new charter sailing business, Amicus Adventure Sailing, was born.

How about that cold trip from Isle Royale? We did make it to shore that night. We pulled in without incident at 9:30 p.m. It had been dark for over three hours already, and it felt like midnight. The children snored below as I steered us flawlessly into the dock. Mark jumped out, stiff and bundled, and secured us.

"And, here we are," he ventured cheerfully. The next morning we woke up to a white world.

Glossary
(by Mark)

Bobstay—cable that holds the bowsprit in place. Great place to hang on and climb while swimming.

Boom—horizontal pole attached to the mast that holds the main sail taut as well as smacks your head if you don't watch out.

Bow—front of the boat.

Bowsprit—the long "fence" that sticks out in front of the boat.

Bulkhead—a wall inside the cabin.

Cockpit—the area in the stern of the boat where you sit and steer.

Depth-sounder—tells you how deep the water is under the boat.

Halyard—rope used to raise the sail.

Harness/tether—the harness attaches around your torso and the tether clips to the harness and then attaches to the boat to keep you from falling overboard.

Hatch—an opening in the deck. There are three hatches on *Amicus*—one at the bow to provide ventilation to the v-berth, one at the stern to provide access to storage at the back of the boat, and the "main hatch" or companionway which is the entrance to the main cabin.

Hatchboard—two clear plexiglas boards that make up the door to the main hatch.

Heeling—the tipping sideways motion of the boat caused by the wind on the sails.

Hull—the main body of the boat.

Intervals (wave)—the time it takes for a wave to travel from crest to crest.

Intracoastal Waterway—a 3000-mile (4800-km) waterway along the Atlantic and Gulf coasts of the United States.

Jacklines—inch wide webbing straps that run the length of the boat on each side of the cabin that are securely attached at the bow and stern. These are what you attach your tether to when working on deck in rough weather.

Jib—the forward-most sail.

Jybing—changing course and the angle of the wind on the sails while sailing downwind.

Kedge anchor—a small anchor used to help pull the boat into deeper water after it has run aground.

Ketch—a sailboat with two masts, the Main (tallest) one in the front and the Mizzen in the back, just forward of the tiller.

Knot—the nautical version of miles per hour; a knot is 1.2 miles per hour.

Lee cloths—cloths attached to the bunk that help keep you in your bunk when sailing in rough weather.

Lifelines—the cables that run along the outside of the deck to help keep you from falling overboard.

Mizzen sail—the sail that attaches to the smaller mast at the stern of the boat.

Netting—looks like fish-net and attaches to the lifelines to help keep the kids from slipping between the lifelines.

Outboard—a small motor that goes on the back of the dinghy.

Piling—wooden post sticking out of the water usually used to tie a boat to.

Portholes—small round windows in the cabin.

Settee—the couch inside the cabin. There is one on the port side and one on the starboard side. The port side one is pulled out to create Mark and Katya's bed—all of thirty-eight inches wide.

Sheet—the rope used to pull in the sails.

Sloop—a sailboat with a single mast.

Staging wall—the wall on the inside of the lock where you prepare to do battle when the lock doors close.